THE ESSENTIAL SKILLS SERIES | BOOK 6

THE POWER
OF AUTHENTICITY

I0078661

Self-help skills for when you feel anxious or depressed

DR. JIMMY HENDERSON

First Published 2025 by Dr Jimmy Henderson
Copyright © 2025 Dr Jimmy Henderson

ISBN 978-0-903733-58-8 (Print)
ISBN 978-0-903733-57-1 (eBook)

Cover and interior crafted with love by the team at
www.myebook.online

MYEBOOK
WE EMPOWER AUTHORS

DISCLAIMER

This publication is not referenced and should not be seen as an authoritative textbook. Anxiety disorders and clinical depression are serious conditions and need the services of a doctor or a psychiatrist if they are to receive the proper treatment and medication. I am therefore not advocating this rational approach as a solution to coping with or resolving anxiety or depression. I am simply hoping to impart some self-help skills to those who are experiencing anxious or depressed feelings or thoughts.

Finally, although every effort is made to ensure efficacy and accuracy, the author, publishers, printers, distributors and/or other related parties do not accept any responsibility whatsoever for any errors or omissions, or effects, arising from this publication.

CREDITS

I wish to thank my publisher, Dave Henderson, of www.myebook.online for his assistance in the completion, publication and marketing of this book.

RESEARCH LINKS

The relevant research articles are listed at the back of the book. You will find other interesting articles on my website:

www.discoveringyourself.co.za

INTRODUCTION

Here is an extract from *The Velveteen Rabbit* by Margery Williams Bianco, which explains, in a delightful way, what it is to be real, genuine and authentic.

'Real isn't how you are made,' said the Skin Horse. 'It's a thing that happens to you. When a child loves you for a long, long time, not just to play with, but really loves you, then you become real.'

'Does it hurt?' asked the Rabbit.

'Sometimes,' said the Skin Horse, for he was always truthful. 'But when you are real you don't mind being hurt.'

'Does it happen all at once, like being wound up,' he asked, 'or bit by bit?'

'It doesn't happen all at once,' said the Skin Horse. 'You become. It takes a long time. That's why it doesn't happen often to people who break easily, or have sharp edges, or who have to be carefully kept. Generally, by the time you are real, most of your hair has been loved off, and your eyes drop out and you get loose in the joints and very shabby. But these things don't matter at all, because once you are real you can't be ugly, except to people who don't understand.'

THE IMPORTANCE OF AUTHENTICITY

I know that there are many reasons for anxiety and depression and also different psychotherapeutic approaches to dealing with these conditions. However, in this book I will be focusing on helping you to rediscover your true self and return to authenticity. My hope is that this will empower you to face up to and hopefully reduce the effect of the unpleasant emotions and thoughts associated with the onset of these conditions.

To answer the question of what authenticity is, I will be working closely with the theory proposed by Dr Donald Winnicott: he believes we have a deeper side to ourselves, an authentic, core self, as opposed to the false sense of self that we create when we are exposed to the conditioning and pressures of life.

In this book I point out the dangers of living inauthentically, which will hopefully help you to see the importance of returning to authentic living. Being alienated from, or out of step with, your authentic self – that which comprises your ethics, highest values and conscience – can result in *cognitive dissonance* and inner conflict, especially if you come to realise this and feel helpless to do anything about it. Such an inner conflict can lead to anxiety and could even be a factor in the development of depression.

Cognitive dissonance is an unpleasant tension that develops in your mind and is caused when your actions do not match your inner values and conscience. This can in turn cause inner turmoil and guilt, and lead to worse conditions such as self-doubt, loneliness, despair, stress, depression and even health problems.

A RATIONAL (COGNITIVE-BEHAVIOURAL THERAPY, OR CBT) APPROACH

In this book I provide self-help guidelines for those of you who are experiencing feelings of anxiety and engaging in the kinds of negative thinking which could lead to depression.

Research has shown a clear connection between a person's emotions and their thinking and actions. Although there are other treatments for feelings of anxiety and depression, as a cognitive scientist I favour a rational (CBT) approach. Following this approach, you will be able to reduce the effects of these conditions by correcting your negative thoughts, self-talk and thinking errors, which often be viewed as being the root causes of anxious thinking.

In line with CBT, this guide book also helps you to develop an action plan for lifestyle changes which will hopefully help you to cope better with your feelings of anxiety and other negative emotions that can lead to depression.

A FOCUSED APPROACH

I have focused my approach on a loss of authenticity and inauthentic living as one of the factors involved in anxiety and the type of negative feelings and thoughts which can eventually lead to depression. I have reformulated simple counselling techniques so that you can apply them yourself and I have framed the processes within case studies as a way of making them easy to follow.

RATIONAL SKILLS

A rational approach is not the same as rationalisation – which is a coping mechanism in which one looks at excuses for not acting in a certain way. In this case, we use rational (cognitive) skills to see through to the actual truth of the matter. This helps us to expose the hidden factors which may explain a person's behaviour in a situation without the distortions to their thinking and perception brought about by powerful negative emotions.

The rational skills included in this book include using the power of hindsight. In this way, forming a more balanced view of an incident is possible when it is viewed after the fact. In addition, the processes of logical reasoning and applying common sense together help to form a more accurate perspective on an incident. The information gathered from these sources is used to challenge errors in thinking such as irrational thoughts, negative self-talk and faulty perceptions, which can lead to the negative feelings linked to anxiety and depression. If these errors can be successfully shown to be false or inaccurate, the emotions can then be released and the healing process can begin.

The aim of the rational approach is ultimately to help you grow and return to authenticity, making it possible for you to cope better with life's challenges and find your way back to your path to personal development.

RESEARCH-BASED CASE STUDIES

Apart from the research cited in the sources section of the book, as mentioned earlier, I use examples of some real-life case studies to show you how to use the processes and follow the correct steps. However, there are other case studies which are hypothetical.

PERSONAL DEVELOPMENT

This is, in essence, a guide book directed at encouraging personal development. Regaining your authenticity can take you further along the road to personal growth, so that you can come to a true realisation of who you really are and of your role and purpose in this life. This will empower you to deal with life's everyday challenges and hopefully make you more resilient when dealing with anxious or depressed feelings and thoughts.

At a higher level, I hope to introduce you to a new world filled with mindfulness, self-insight, meaning and purpose. I hope, too, that any new insights you gain through this book will help you to become whole and 'real' again.

I also hope that, after reading this guide, you will be able to heal outstanding issues in your life and move forward with confidence to reach that state of mind called *self-actualisation* by psychologists such as Goldstein, Maslow and Rogers. This means becoming what you are capable of being. In other words, it translates into your realising and fulfilling your full potential.

I wish you all the best in your reading of this book.

CONTENTS

CHAPTER 1
WHAT IS AUTHENTICITY?

THE TRUE SELF AND THE FALSE SELF

Donald Winnicott, a British paediatrician and psychoanalyst, introduced the idea of all of us having both a 'true self' and a 'false' sense of self.

According to Winnicott, the true self represents the authentic and spontaneous core of an individual. It is the innate and genuine aspect of a person, reflecting their true beliefs, values, feelings and innermost desires, almost a childlike state ruled by our conscience. This is the real 'us', a rational centre built on reason, common sense, honesty and the capacity to care, to love and be loved. Unfortunately, during the course of our lives, this true self is usually covered up and surrounded by a multitude of anxieties, tensions and other unhelpful emotions plus layer upon layer of misguided thoughts.

THE ANALOGY OF A HURRICANE

I can compare this to being in the midst of a powerful hurricane of swirling emotions and irrational thoughts. Within the hurricane we find the whirling winds and raging storms of life which bring us nothing but worries, tensions and concerns that make us anxious. But if we are prepared to seek further and search deep enough within ourselves, we will find an area of peace, calm and self-love, the eye of the hurricane, our true, authentic selves.

THE FALSE SELF

In contrast, the 'false self' is just a socially acceptable fake mask (a façade or a coping mechanism) which we create in a world in which appearances are everything. It is a world in which we are conditioned to meet the demands and expectations of our families, friends, careers – and even of society itself.

The relationship between the different levels of our psyche can be more clearly explained if I use another analogy – the layers of our skin:

- The top layer is like the false sense of self which is visible to others and is normally accepted as the actual person, but what you are seeing is only on the surface.
- The middle layer is like our authentic self, containing most of the important parts like the blood vessels, nerves and sensory neurons. If something goes wrong here, it has far more serious implications.
- The bottom or fatty layer could be seen as the subconscious parts of our self, which is concealed from view and contains all our hidden programmes, desires,

conditioning and memories that unconsciously influence our actions.

THE FALSE SELF IN SOCIETY

We are actually living in a metaphoric global web of deception and delusion created by those who wish to influence, condition, control and manipulate others. This can be seen in politics, advertising, marketing, mainstream news outlets and social media. Here, greed, deception and hidden agendas are ever present. In a world like this, we normal people become pawns in a game played by those who wield power and influence.

As children, we learn to live and adjust to living in such a world, often blissfully unaware of what is happening behind the scenes, while our innocence, our true sense of self and our rational core is slowly being eroded. Eventually we become an empty shell, a false sense of self, conditioned to act according to the dictates of society, having lost the ability to think and act spontaneously.

The problem is that most of the time we don't even know that we have been conditioned, and this is why it is so insidious. In order to play according to the rules of the game of this world, we often give up our independent thinking and personal values. We are expected to cover up how we actually feel about an issue and go with the majority, repress what we really think and believe, and conform to what is expected of us. Eventually, this leads to our conscience being silenced or at least muted – one of the effects of a lost sense of authenticity.

However, at some point in our lives we may begin to feel an inner conflict and feelings of anxiety, which eventually filters through to affect our mental health and well-being, as, at a deep level, we know we are not acting according to our true nature and best intentions.

This is our authentic self prompting us to look within and deal with these contradictions.

The problem is that, once we create this false sense of self, our ethics, values and priorities begin to change, and we begin to choose careers over families, money over integrity and social acceptance over truth and honour. This false sense of self, in turn, then becomes ego-driven, essentially self-seeking and selfish.

A SOCIAL COMMENTARY

In our current society, this may seem normal and necessary, because we are only seeking what most people want: prestige, money, power and position. And are these not the measure of success in this modern world? However, this is where the first level of deception arises.

In a world such as this with its skewed priorities, it is so easy to become alienated from our own inner truth. As a result, the costs of giving up our authenticity are not so clear in the beginning. It is only when we begin to see the effects of this artificial state of mind on our family and especially our emotional, psychological and physical health that we may come to realise that we have compromised our integrity and sold out our conscience for the sake of a few pieces of silver. And then we begin to realise that the illusion of the false self has taken over our lives.

For us to realise what is actually going on, it normally takes a wake-up call in the form of a traumatic or an unpleasant experience or a nasty series of events in which our whole sense of self is threatened – if, that is, we have the self-awareness and the insight to do so.

In other words, even life's hard knocks could serve a purpose: that of calling us to reassess ourselves and our lives. If you start to see life's challenges in this light, you may be back on your path to authenticity.

One of the aims of this book is to give you the skills you need to awaken from your slumber of conditioning, to help you to realise how you have been deceived (or even fooled yourself) and to offer you a new path back to who you were meant to be: an authentic, real and genuine human being. This will help you to rediscover the true meaning and purpose of your life and find out what true success is: not money and prestige, but honesty, truth and fully conscious living.

CHAPTER 2
THE IMPORTANCE OF AUTHENTICITY

n this chapter, I reveal to you the real reasons why being 'real' or 'authentic' is important in all aspects of our lives. However, before I do this, I need you to understand exactly what I mean by being authentic and why it is so important to your mental and emotional health.

EXPLAINING AUTHENTICITY

US President Joe Biden is quoted as saying in his inaugural address that we can take pride in honesty, directness and expressing our true selves, even if it is out of fashion. Here he was speaking about authenticity, or being authentic and 'real', genuine and trustworthy.

Authenticity is about being honest with yourself and others and acting according to your true conscience, beliefs, feelings and values. It's the opposite of being deceptive or false. When you are 'real' or authentic, you don't wear masks, deceive people or pretend to be someone other than who you truly are. You have real insight into yourself and your values, beliefs and ethics, and are prepared to act accordingly. In other words, there is no conflict between what you say and what you feel and how you act.

Because there is no inner conflict, your conscience is clear, with the result that you don't carry around any subconscious guilt or have any underlying anxieties. This also means that your core or centre of self consists of rational thinking and has not been shaped and distorted by social conditioning or polluted by doubts, fears, worries and concerns. Your motives are pure and you can sleep peacefully at night.

Authenticity is actually part of the larger process of human self-development and self-actualisation, which can take a long time to fully unfold. However, as I have pointed out, it can easily be lost in the hustle and bustle of everyday life amid pressures from work, home and society itself. As a result, regaining your authenticity once it is forgotten can be difficult and it requires a lot more effort.

SIGNS OF AUTHENTICITY

Psychologists Michael Kernis and Brian Goldman pointed out four key factors that point to the fact that you are living an authentic life:

- **Self-awareness (or mindfulness):** You have insight into your self and you trust your good intentions and motives, the accuracy of what you truly feel, and your choices. This level of self-knowledge gives you confidence in your abilities.

- **Objectivity (a lack of bias):** You are able to look at things in an unbiased way as there are no hidden factors that can subconsciously influence you. This makes your thinking clear and you are objectively able to evaluate both your strengths and weaknesses and the facts that are placed before you. There is no self-deception, denial or being unduly influenced from outside. Being without bias also means that you are fair and honest in your dealings with others and treat one and all equally.
- **Congruency:** You act in ways which match your true identity, feelings, values and needs and can resist criticism or rejection by others. This indicates a high degree of resilience, self-confidence, self-esteem and belief in yourself.
- **Good relationships:** You are open and honest in your relationships. You come across as a reasonable person who is unconditionally accepting of others and who is not afraid to show your vulnerability. Research shows that authentic people are kinder, more compassionate and more caring towards others.

I will be focusing on these four key growth areas given by Kernis and Goldman, which will hopefully help you to return to authenticity and better manage both your anxieties and any negative depressed feelings you may have.

COMMENT

However, I first want to add another factor to the four already given by Kernis and Goldman: that of authenticity being able to help you with your conscious personal growth.

CONSCIOUS PERSONAL GROWTH

I believe that authenticity also means being willing and able to follow your passion. And that it is intimately connected to unfolding your natural abilities, strengths and talents, and that this can help to promote your personal growth and development as a person.

The reason for this is that being authentic means that you have a high degree of self-awareness, mindfulness and self-insight, plus the self-knowledge necessary for healthy personal growth and development. This self-awareness helps you to perform self-introspection and self-analysis, during which you could find aspects of yourself that need to be worked at. In this case, the rational thinking also linked to authenticity will allow you to take active steps to deal with these issues, such as going for counselling, coaching or attending personal growth courses. Authentic people are open and honest and therefore not afraid to seek help if they need it.

Without the self-awareness provided by authenticity, you could remain in the dark (or in denial) about those aspects of your personality that need development, and in this way you may never achieve self-actualisation. In truly knowing yourself, you can build a sense of confidence, independence and self-motivation that opens the doors to real growth and empowerment, after which you will no longer be at the mercy of circumstances and can become the master of your own life.

LIVING WITH AUTHENTICITY

I now discuss these five key growth areas in more detail and show you how living with authenticity has the potential to help you manage your life better and in this way reduce both anxiety and any possible negative or depressing tendencies.

SELF-AWARENESS AND MINDFULNESS

Being mindful means that you are more open to self-introspection and self-insight and as a result have a better chance of knowing who you really are, what you can be (your true potential) and what you want to do with your life. This sense of purpose and direction is important for your future. If you don't know what you want and where you are going, or if you don't have specific goals, you are less likely to advance in your life.

AUTHENTICITY BRINGS SELF-KNOWLEDGE

Knowing who you are inside, and having definite ethics and values, means that you are more open and confident, less defensive and more self-accepting. This does not necessarily mean that all authentic people are saints. But self-knowledge and self-insight gives you a distinct advantage over others who are still trying to figure out who they are, what their priorities are in life and what life means to them.

AUTHENTICITY HELPS WITH SELF-CONFIDENCE

Authenticity offers you a level of psychological integration with which you're able to build your self-confidence and inner strength in a way that helps you cope better with challenges at home and in business relationships. This confidence will also assist in your decision-making, which leads to your gaining more meaning and enjoying greater success in your life. In other words, you aren't so influenced by the opinions of others and society's expectations, because you know yourself and exactly what you want and need in your life and can make decisions accordingly.

AUTHENTICITY IMPROVES YOUR SELF-IMAGE

Your self-image can be explained as who you see (or believe) yourself to be. In other words, what do you see when you look in the mirror and what do you believe about yourself? As someone who is genuine and true? Or as someone who has lost their way? Knowing who and what you are comes from being authentic. This should allow you to build a more positive self-image because you have accepted yourself, warts and all.

AUTHENTICITY IMPROVES YOUR SELF-ESTEEM

Research has shown that authenticity also builds self-esteem. Self-esteem is the way you feel about yourself. In other words, your feelings of self-worth. The problem here is that your self-esteem can be influenced by what others think and have to say about you and whether these comments are positive and uplifting or negative and destructive. Once again, if you are authentic, you have nothing to hide and can resist threats to your self-esteem. Bolstered by your self-esteem, you're certain about who you are and won't allow the opinions of others to influence the way you feel about yourself.

Furthermore, knowing yourself and your true strengths and weaknesses allows you to act with greater self-understanding and therefore with more decisiveness and confidence. And when it is combined with mindfulness and logical reasoning, self-esteem will also help you make better decisions, which will in turn improve your feelings of self-worth even more.

AUTHENTICITY BRINGS MEANING AND PURPOSE

It has been shown that it's the meaning and purpose gained by living authentically which gives the authentic person an advantage over others. If you absolutely know what you really want out of life and set the right goals, it can bring meaning and purpose into your life. It was Henry Kissinger who said: 'If you do not know where you are going, every road will get you nowhere.' Without this self-knowledge and the resulting sense of direction, you will simply remain reactive and respond to things as they happen – and be tossed around like a cork in the sea.

AUTHENTICITY PROMOTES RATIONALITY

One of the most important attributes of the authentic self is rationality. In fact, it is often referred to as your *rational core*. Being rational is the ability to think with clarity, common sense and reason. In other words, you are more likely to be a conscious thinking person, one who is able to set aside the conditioning that normally obscures your thinking processes. In this way, you are better equipped to manage your life, make good decisions and plan effectively. This mental clarity will also help you to see and avoid situations which could cause anxiety or weigh you down emotionally.

AUTHENTICITY CLEARS THE WAY FOR LOGICAL THINKING

A spin-off of this clarity and rationality is logical thinking. A more logical approach to life will allow you to deal effectively with life's irritations, challenges and obstacles, helping to reduce your level of anxiety and to combat negative thoughts and feelings.

Logical thinking will also help you develop an ability to think critically. This ability will empower you to reason more effectively, think more independently and apply your common sense to see the truth through the webs of falsity, manipulation and deceit that are so pervasive in this world. These are all issues that will introduce anxiety into your life and lead you down the path to negative thinking. To learn how to develop good logical thinking and reasoning, read my book titled *Critical thinking*.

AUTHENTICITY PUTS YOU IN TOUCH WITH YOUR TRUE IDENTITY

Like super-heroes, we sometimes cover up our true identities to fit in or so as to not be judged.

Getting in touch with your true identity may be confusing at first, though, as you may be surprised to find out that your real persona is not what you expected. For example, some people cover up their lack of self-esteem or introversion by trying to be the life of the party, the person who always tells the best jokes. However, in this case, the clown is hiding his true pain behind his painted face and mask. I have seen this happen many times.

Some people may come to realise that they have been living a lie regarding their sexual orientation or even their gender. 'Coming out of the closet' could be seen as acknowledging one's authentic self, and it could even be said that people who come to terms with being transgender believe that their true self (that is, their gender identity) has been denied all these years.

OBJECTIVITY: A LACK OF BIAS

Research on authenticity has shown that it is vital for discovering the meaning in your life and also or your optimal psychological functioning. Knowing that you are acting in an objective, open, transparent, unbiased and honest manner with integrity brings with it a sense of well-being and, as I said earlier, it builds a positive self-image and healthy self-esteem. This, in turn, results in more confidence, resilience, a greater capacity for independent thinking and self-acceptance, and also greater tolerance towards others. In other words, if you are authentic and confident in yourself, another person's attitude towards you won't upset you and you can avoid being biased towards them.

When you are 'real', there are no hidden agendas or factors that can influence you subconsciously. This makes your thinking clear and you are objectively able to evaluate both situations and your own strengths and weaknesses. There is no self-deception or self-denial, and no inner tensions or conflicts, and this leads to much-improved mental and physical health.

CONGRUENCY

Congruency is a term used by Carl Rogers (a humanistic psychologist) to describe a state in which a person's ideal (authentic) self and their actual thoughts, emotions and actions are consistent or very similar. In other words, there is a good integration and mutual sharing of information between their emotional and their psychological systems. Counsellors and other therapists often have to build or develop congruency in order to deal with the often very demanding task of working with the intense emotions of clients.

Congruency means that you are not easily shaken because you have a coherent match or balance between the different parts of your psyche. This gives you an inner resilience that renders you impervious to emotional attack, criticism or rejection by others. It is almost like wearing a suit of armour.

It also seems that congruent people are less prone to anxiety or self-doubt, are more resilient in the face of peer pressure and are able to cope better with the ups and downs of everyday life. Being more integrated, they are able to make quick and confident choices, to think independently – and they certainly don't need the approval of others.

You may have heard it said that someone has it 'all together', which means that they have a stable, balanced approach to life. This suggests congruency and authenticity.

CONGRUENCY KEEPS YOU GROUNDED

If you are congruent, you are fully grounded and have a better chance of managing your feelings of anxiety rather than being controlled by them. This grounding also inclines you to be more pragmatic and helps you to understand why you are caught up in an insidious web of emotions; it also enables you to take the necessary steps to unravel them. This groundedness will also give you strength and direction during the difficult times.

GOOD RELATIONSHIPS

Authenticity also means that you are open and honest in your relationships. You come across as a reasonable person who is tolerant and unconditionally accepting of others and also as someone who is not afraid to show their vulnerability. Authentic people strive to be kinder, more compassionate and caring towards others.

In addition, authentic people are more optimistic and positive in their approach to life and altruistic in their actions towards others: they are certainly not false. They have the clear conscience that goes with being 'real'.

Moving from inauthenticity to authenticity helps you to be more confident and assertive. Assertiveness is not a negative trait and does not mean that you are a difficult person. On the contrary, it points to your ability to present your point of view with confidence, and this can be a good quality in establishing relationships based on mutual respect.

In fact, in our relationships, being assertive has the following benefits:

- It restores your 'personal power', which you need for self-confidence.
- It helps you to manage your emotions during personal altercations.
- It improves your self-image and self-esteem, which means that you earn the respect of others.

CONSCIOUS PERSONAL GROWTH

As I said previously, I have added a fifth factor to the previous four, that of conscious personal growth, because I believe is also dependent on living authentically. There are a number of areas in which this growth will be most noticeable.

AUTHENTICITY GIVES YOU THE POWER TO TAKE PERSONAL RESPONSIBILITY FOR YOUR LIFE

The independent thinking that comes with authenticity means that you know and accept that you have the freedom to choose. In other words, you are willing to break away from the conditioning of society and to take responsibility not only for your choices, but also for your own conscious personal growth. These qualities will improve your ability to cope with everyday life, your confidence in your abilities to make good decisions, and your ability to respond and adapt effectively to change. This opens the door to self-actualisation.

AUTHENTICITY IS NECESSARY ON THE PATH TO SELF-ACTUALISATION

Personal development is a natural process in which we pass through various stages of growth, maturing emotionally and psychologically until we (hopefully) reach the highest state of self-actualisation. I explained this earlier as meeting our full potential in giving expression to our God-given talents, showing honesty and integrity and unfolding the best parts of our character.

Authenticity is essential for self-actualisation, otherwise it is only our false sense of self that is growing and probably moving us further away from our true core selves. In essence, if we don't know, understand, meet or satisfy our true needs and dreams, our chances of attaining self-actualisation are virtually zero. It is only through true authenticity that we can ever unfold the best and finest version of ourselves. This certainly sounds like a great goal and purpose to strive for in life.

CHAPTER 3
HOW WE LOSE OUR AUTHENTICITY

Although it seems like such a small matter, losing our authenticity can create long-term problems for our personal development, our advancement in life and our general well-being. The problems begin when we become alienated or lose contact with our true self, for whatever reason, as this is the part of our psyche that keeps us balanced, rational and aligned with our highest good.

Unfortunately, there are many influences and distractions in the world that can turn our attention away from this deep awareness of our self. Some of them begin in childhood and kick in others when we enter adolescence or later in the adult world, when we become caught up in the complexity of work, family life and business, and social and intimate relationships.

A number of specific factors can lead to a loss of authenticity and cause anxiety. I therefore take this opportunity to point them out and discuss them here:

INHERITED TRAITS

Your anxiety could be due to the personality and physical traits you have inherited – which, in fact, is really not any fault of yours. For example, many people who suffer from anxiety are often very conscious and sensitive. Being a sensitive person is not necessarily a bad thing or a curse; it just means that you are very self-aware and open to what is going on around you. Being sensitive is necessary for creative people, such as artists, poets, musicians and writers. The problem arises when you cannot manage or direct your sensitivity in a crazy or confusing world, and this can result in your alienation from society and lead to the kinds of thoughts and beliefs which lead to anxiety.

Unfortunately, children can be predisposed to nasty personality traits which they inherit from their parents. Under the right circumstances, and without appropriate guidance, they could easily relinquish their authenticity. For example, some children seem to be born with certain vulnerabilities that open them up to manipulation and deception and they then fall into the habit of lying and deceiving others in order to stay out of trouble or to make money.

CASE STUDY

Ashley is extremely clever, but also manipulative and convincing, a trait he seems to have inherited from his father, who left the family when he was young. He has now become a computer whiz kid and is mixed up with a group of online scammers. Ashley doesn't even seem bothered by the fact that he is targeting and defrauding older people on the internet who are not tech-savvy, and he says it is their own fault that they are so gullible. This suggests that he has sold out his authenticity and his conscience in pursuit of greed.

Here is another case study which relates to other inherited traits and the consequences they can also lead to.

CASE STUDY

Melody has a problem with her weight, a trait she inherited from her parents, who are also both obese. As a result, she now has low self-esteem and is also very self-conscious socially. These two factors combine to render her prone to peer pressure. She is always eager to please and will always go along with her friends, even if they engage in risky activities, such as underage drinking and drugs. Unfortunately, this means that she is sacrificing her true self, her own set of values and even her conscience just to be accepted.

Melody feels uncomfortable when participating in such activities, but her drive and need to be accepted override her rational thinking, and this creates inner conflict and anxiety. To try to cope with these anxieties, she goes on eating binges and is now also bulimic.

CONDITIONING

The second most common way of losing your authenticity is through the normal process of conditioning that takes place in homes, businesses and society as a whole. Conditioning can be explained as influencing and shaping other people's thinking and behaviour, usually with the promise of rewards or the threat of punishment.

The original idea behind conditioning may have been noble: for instance, instilling discipline in children and bringing people into line with certain rules and laws with a view to keeping the peace, maintaining balance and promoting growth in society. However, this original ideal is easily corrupted by those who have their own reasons and agendas for wanting to move the masses in a certain direction. In this regard, read my previous book titled *Critical thinking*.

This process of conditioning begins in childhood, where well-meaning parents impose discipline on their children using rewards and punishment in order to get them to meet acceptable standards of social behaviour. In children there is also another form of conditioning called modelling, where they simply follow the example set by their parents.

Unfortunately, in this way, parents can transfer their own issues, problems, prejudices, skewed beliefs and dysfunctional behaviours on to their children, as will be seen in subsequent case studies.

TRYING TO CONFORM

I think it is natural that most children will try to fulfil the expectations of their parents or caregivers. This means that they can be conditioned to adopt beliefs, values, attitudes and behaviours which are truly not their own. And if these ideas do not match up to the child's real-life experiences, this can cause confusion, with children ending up losing their individuality and covering up their true nature in an attempt to conform, to be accepted or simply to cope with the challenges at home, especially those that characterise a dysfunctional family. This kind of confusion can lead to childhood insecurities, which is another way of losing one's child-like innocence and authenticity.

CASE STUDY

This is the sad case of Johnny, a child who brought up in a home environment where prejudice and discrimination were openly practised and encouraged by his parents. Johnny was actually a sensitive child. Consequently, the inner conflict between what he had been told to do and how to behave towards others, on the one hand, and what he innately felt to be wrong, on the other, caused him extreme distress, guilt and anxiety. It took many years before Johnny was able to undo the damage that had been done to his fragile psyche and become whole again – and be able to act according to the dictates of his conscience.

CHILDHOOD INSECURITIES

Children will become anxious at an early age if there is instability in their home environment. This could be the result of confusion or insecurity stemming from problems in the family such as parental conflict, divorce, an absent father figure, a shortage of money or some other form of neglect. Children need guidance from an early age, otherwise they will struggle to form a balanced personality and stay in touch with their authentic selves.

These insecurities usually result in low self-esteem, which will only further complicate matters. Eventually, the child will not know what to believe or to do and could, in fact, in bad cases, even 'lose themselves' by withdrawing into a form of childhood depression.

CHILDHOOD DRAMA

Unfortunately, experiences of childhood trauma can also lead to low self-esteem and self-isolation, which is a recipe for anxiety and childhood depression.

CASE STUDY

Thomas's father left the family just before he became an adolescent, and Thomas hardly saw him after that. His father never bothered to take him out again or share quality time with him. Thomas told himself that he was coping, but he was constantly ill and withdrawn. He felt that his father had abandoned him, although his struggling mother did her best to give him the support that he needed. The problem was that he had three other brothers who were younger than him and they needed more of his mother's attention. As a result, he felt very alone and isolated during his teenage years.

Although he did not outwardly show it, Thomas felt very insecure, as the family were also poor, surviving only on the small maintenance that their father provided. The teenager's self-esteem, confidence and social life suffered as a result. He was also unable to express how he really felt, and did not know who he really was or what he wanted from life. He had no plan for his future and became alienated from the person he was born to be.

Fortunately, Thomas entered the armed services, and those experiences and discipline 'cleansed' his personality, which meant that he was able eventually to rediscover his authentic self. Unfortunately, not everyone is as fortunate as Thomas, and I know of many who have been lost in the inauthenticity of this modern world.

CHILDHOOD NEGLECT AND ABUSE

Thomas's story is still nothing compared to those of others who have had even more horrendous childhoods, such as youngsters who have experienced physical or emotional abuse and even abandonment or neglect. Such children may have lived in constant fear and tension, not knowing what to expect at home, or even when it would happen again. The worst of it all was the thought that parents are supposed to be those closest to you, those who support you and whom you love and trust. But a drunken or a drugged-up, abusive father or mother can easily engender chronic feelings of mistrust, fear, insecurity, nervousness and anxiety. This can cause such confusion in the minds of children that they do not know who they really are any more.

SOCIETAL PRESSURES

Even for those children who have a stable family life, society itself can place undue pressure on them to perform and these pressures can contribute to feelings of stress or anxiety and a loss of connection with their innocence, their inner stability or their true self.

PERFORMANCE ANXIETY

For example, certain cultures place very strong emphasis on performance. This result in children experiencing great pressure to meet parental, cultural or societal expectations, such as achieving high grades or being successful in their careers. This can also lead to anxiety that arises from a fear of failure. These expectations can also lead to a choice of career which may not be their own, resulting in alienation from their true feelings, needs, wants and desires.

CASE STUDY

I recall research that I conducted many years ago for an NGO into teenage suicides involving young girls in a certain area of Durban, South Africa. My interviews with parents, teachers and adolescent girls revealed that the girls felt that they were under tremendous pressure from their parents and their culture to perform academically and to pursue careers which afforded them a high status and income, such as doctors, lawyers and accountants, even though this was not really their choice. This had led to extreme anxiety, teenage depression and a spate of suicides.

PRESSURES ON YOUNG ADULTS

PEER PRESSURE

Even without parental pressure, the physical and emotional changes that occur during adolescence can be a major time of confusion for teenagers and lead to separation from their authentic selves. For instance, teenagers will go to great lengths to gain social acceptance from their peers and stronger personalities can easily influence them into performing acts which go against their true nature. If these friends have links to crime or gangs, this can be a serious problem.

CASE STUDY

Vincent is a young man from a very poor neighbourhood in a major city. His father left home when he was very young and he now battles with low-self-esteem, anxiety and insecurities. The neighbourhood is rife with gangs and his struggling mother has tried unsuccessfully to keep him away from drugs and violence. By joining a gang, Vincent believes he has now found acceptance and respect, but what he does not realise is that the price of doing so has been a loss of his true self and the opportunity to actualise himself fully. He also runs the risk of run-ins with the law, which could ruin his life further.

THE MEDIA

Social pressure is not limited to family and friends. For example, the media and advertising also play a role in creating this idealisation of a 'perfect' body and the 'highly successful young adult' in advertising and in films and this can lead to dissatisfaction and anxiety among young people who feel concerned about their physical appearance or lack of achievement. This could be one of the reasons for the increase in plastic surgery procedures and an obsession with the body beautiful, in addition to the many anxieties and insecurities that we see in young people today.

TRYING TO IMPRESS OTHERS

Insecure young adults will create a false sense of self to try to match what they see on television or in the films as 'cool' when, in fact, it may go against their very nature. In this way they alienate themselves from their authentic inner core even further.

For example, it is quite common for young men to lie and pretend to be wealthy and successful in order to impress and attract the ladies. The same could also be said of young women who dress up and lie about their age, social standing and connections. Social masks are quite common in societies where money, prestige and status are sought-after commodities. However, this means that these individuals may lose touch with their true inner selves.

CAUSES OF INAUTHENTICITY IN ADULTS

Apart from the problems that arise in childhood, there are also issues which arise later in adult life that could result in people losing touch with their true authentic selves.

POOR LIVING CONDITIONS

In adults, a low self-esteem and alienation from the self can arise as a result of having to take care of families in a debilitating environment filled with poverty, unemployment and social rejection. Such conditions lead to humiliation, self-doubt and insecurity, which can prompt adults to also seek acceptance and respect. Their doing so in turn opens them up to being easily influenced to do things which they would normally not do, such as participating in gangsterism and crime. These actions in turn alienate them further from themselves, to the point where they are eventually entirely disconnected from the promptings of their consciences.

LOW SELF-ESTEEM

As mentioned previously, low self-esteem can render even adults susceptible to peer pressure. This can be explained as being influenced to do something in a group which you would normally not do if you were alone. Its power relates to our social needs to be accepted (loved) and respected, and also a fear of social exclusion, isolation or rejection.

To anyone with a low self-esteem, stronger personalities or authority figures can be very persuasive. The problem is that not everyone has the same morals or value systems and therefore bad influences can introduce you to nasty situations such as drug and alcohol abuse, violence or even crime. These are activities that probably don't conform to your beliefs, values, morality or conscience at all, which can result in your feeling guilt and experiencing inner conflict. This will widen the gap between you and your authentic self. And over time this guilt and stress can wear you down and you may even spiral down into depression.

ADULT CONDITIONING AND RIGID THINKING

Even as adults we can lose our spontaneity and authenticity by being conditioned to become part of a system designed to control instead of to assist, empower and develop members of society. Here I am thinking of the bureaucratic systems to which we are exposed every day in which unthinking people hide behind a book of instructions and rigid rules and regulations instead of using their own minds to think for themselves, in addition to not acting altruistically, creatively or spontaneously.

An example of this would be the public servant or corporate consultant who turns down the application of an elderly person and sends them away based on a technicality or something which could be easily solved with only a bit of effort, a phone call or an email.

In other words, how many people will go the extra mile to help someone who, for whatever reason, doesn't quite meet their rigid requirements involving mere paperwork? Authentic and conscientious people would. As I mentioned earlier, research has shown that authentic people are prepared to move beyond expectations, they being generally kinder, more tolerant, ethical and caring towards others. Being complete in themselves, they do not have to put others down to boost their own self-esteem.

SACRIFICING AUTHENTICITY FOR POWER, PRESTIGE OR MONEY

Many people are prepared to sacrifice their integrity and authenticity in pursuit of success, power and money. This is especially true in the case of politics, where manipulation, double-dealing, deception and the masking of one's true intentions, motives and feelings are the tools most used to move ahead.

Another case of sacrificing authenticity for gain would be a hedonistic lifestyle of continuous partying and distractions, where you don't allow yourself the time for genuine self-examination and a consideration of important questions such as the meaning and purpose of your life. Once you give up your self-awareness in the pursuit of money or pleasure, the chances are that you'll lose your connection to your authentic self.

CASE STUDY

Clive had always wanted to be successful, having plenty of money. Working long hours, he was eventually promoted to human resources director. Although he had a great position, he was, in reality, not really a people person and struggled with the work that the position required of him. He eventually realised that it was the prestige and salary of this high-powered position that he wanted, but in order to get the promotion he had put forward a façade or a false self, and the type of work did not suit his temperament or abilities at all. This realisation led to much inner conflict and anxiety and his health also suffered as a result.

This can happen to many people who take on job roles for which they are not suited, simply for the sake of the elevated salary and position. The reality, though, is that this inauthenticity and falsity will eventually catch up with them in some way, as they have become disconnected from their true selves. Such a development can lead to these inner conflicts, tensions and anxiety. For example, individuals in such positions live in constant fear of being exposed as hypocrites, deceivers or even liars, as they can't continue to cover up their incompetencies or indiscretions.

If they go too deep into this life of deception, they may eventually forget who they really are and go through life continually searching for that elusive state of happiness.

INCONSISTENCIES BETWEEN THINKING AND ACTION

Sometimes we are put in difficult situations where we have to make a choice as to our values, what we believe and what we are obliged to do in our lives or in our work situation. This can lead to inner turmoil, sometimes at a subconscious level, and it can bring with it anxiety and alienation from our true selves.

CASE STUDY

Susan follows a religious belief system that does not support abortion. However, she is actually pro-choice in the case of abortion. In other words, she embraces the idea that a woman should be able to have an abortion if she so wishes. Consequently, whenever Susan attends a church service in which abortion is condemned, she feels very uncomfortable and anxious. She is sensing the incongruency between her personal conviction and her religious beliefs and this causes cognitive dissonance, confused feelings and anxiety.

INCONGRUENCY BETWEEN OBLIGATIONS AND CONSCIENCE

Once again, the lack of congruency between what one believes and one's work, social or family obligations can lead to inner tensions, confusion and a loss of authenticity.

CASE STUDY

Jane had recently been promoted and given a very high-level position in human resources management. However, the job role requires that she take on the responsibility of retrenching excess staff. This doesn't suit her quiet, sensitive and caring personality and she begins to experience stress and anxiety as she knows instinctively that she is not being true to her inner nature and conscience.

Jane soon begins to experience panic attacks. After a few months, she begins to experience major acid reflux and stomach pain, which makes her life unbearable and as a result she has to see a gastro-intestinal specialist. Eventually, her illness comes to the attention of her directors and she is moved to another position in which she is able to be more herself and act authentically. She is one of the fortunate ones.

HOW DO YOU KNOW WHEN YOU ARE LOSING YOUR AUTHENTICITY?

Here are a number of guidelines that point to a lack of authenticity. If you see these danger signs in your thinking and actions, take steps to reconcile yourself.

YOU HAVE UNCOMFORTABLE FEELINGS

- If you feel uncomfortable about your decisions and actions, this could be due to an inner conflict or the cognitive dissonance I wrote about earlier. This is a signal from your authentic or true self that you are out of synchronicity with your true values and feelings on the matter.
- You feel embarrassed by things you've done or said, and this points to a lack of self-confidence. This is often associated with the self-doubt brought on by knowing that you may have acted against your better judgement and are not being 'real' at all. In other words, you have acted inauthentically.
- You feel awkward and self-conscious when meeting others, because you know you are pretending to be someone you are not and are afraid that they will see through your façade.
- You may feel guilty or resentful, because you know you are being coerced into doing something or agreeing with someone else just to conform or please them, rather than

speaking your own truth. For example, this could arise when your boss asks your opinion about a terrible idea and you support them simply because you want to be accepted and not antagonise them.

- You are constantly afraid of what others think of you, because you realise you are living a lie and they may find out.
- You have built-up tensions in your body which are causing health problems. These tensions may be signs of inner conflict between different parts of your personality.

IGNORING WARNINGS FROM YOUR 'INNER VOICE'

Learn to listen to your inner voice. Doubtful thoughts are another signal from your authentic self. You should have a little voice inside your head which will warn you that 'this isn't who I am'. These are promptings or wake-up calls from your subconscious that something is amiss. This could happen especially in instances of peer pressure, where you are being encouraged to do something that goes against your true nature.

EXAMPLES

The following are a number of examples of actions that warn you of a possible alienation from your true self or a lack of authenticity. These all relate back to the possible causes of inauthentic behaviour mentioned in the previous section:

- Hiding behind rules and regulations instead of thinking for yourself
- Unethical actions

- Inconsistencies between your actions and your beliefs and values
- Conforming to the demands of others even when you don't agree with them
- Making decisions which go against your conscience
- Not being true to your core values, beliefs and convictions in order to gain power, prestige or money.

CHAPTER 4
THE RESULTS OF INAUTHENTIC LIVING

INNER TENSIONS AND HEALTH ISSUES

Research shows that authentic living can lead to better psychological and physical health. For example, a study in the *Journal of Counselling Psychology* found that authenticity correlates with higher self-esteem, psychological well-being and happiness. Stated differently, inauthentic living can slow down your attempts at achieving mental and emotional wellness.

Being alienated from your rational core can lead to mental confusion and cognitive dissonance as you lose contact with that coherent part of yourself. This can also lead to anxiety and, over the long term, it can a factor in developing depression.

Inner conflict takes place when different components of a person's personality are in opposition to each other. For example, a conflict between one's conscience and a basic drive such as greed. Studies have shown that deep-seated conflicts can cause anxiety, which, in turn, worsens already-present medical problems.

For example, if anxiety, tensions and negative feelings are not dealt with, the stress can build up and lead to the kind of health issues that result from *hypertension,* such as heart attacks, strokes and other organ failures.

LOSING CONTACT WITH YOUR RATIONAL SELF

Your authentic self is the most rational part of your psyche, so if you lose contact with this source of rationality, you won't be able to think objectively about any situation or even recognise repressed emotions such as anger, resentment or depressed feelings. This will prevent you from dealing with these emotions or finding solutions to challenges in your life. As a result, you will react to situations as they arise, without any proactive insight or planning on your part. And if you can't think proactively, or with mindfulness, you will simply act on your immediate desires or, even worse, on those negative emotions.

You need self-insight and a good understanding of what's going on inside your mind and with your emotions in order to make sense of what is happening in your life; what's more, a good understanding will enable you to see the possible causes of your problems and to do something about them. In other words, you have to be able to critically evaluate your situation, your challenges and also your strengths and weaknesses if you are to make good decisions, deal with your problems and still experience conscious personal growth. If you lose access to your rational core, this will not be possible.

A LOSS OF DIRECTION, MEANING AND PURPOSE

A sense of direction, meaning and purpose is essential to authentic living and is also necessary if you are to break free from feelings of depression. One of the most important aspects of authenticity is knowing yourself and what you really want to do with your life. Being disconnected from your true dreams, desires, needs and aspirations can result in a loss of meaning and purpose in your life. If you are continually influenced by other people in doing what they want, you could lose what little self-understanding and control you still have and therefore end up without direction.

Having direction, meaning and purpose in your life is also essential to confident living and personal growth. If you lose sight of these three signposts along the way, you could end up floundering in an ocean of anxiety, doubt and uncertainty and put yourself on the road to depression.

GIVING UP YOUR IDENTITY

The meaning and purpose in your life is often linked to your identity. A loss of identity can come about as a result of social conditioning in which you deny your true self and begin to behave in a way that you believe the world will find more acceptable.

For example, as a strong, independent woman you should know what you want from life. But if you are just conforming and accepting gender injustices to fit in and be accepted, your authenticity, state of mind and health will eventually suffer.

This outcome will be even worse if you come from a strong cultural background, as you may experience a disconnection from your roots and begin letting go of your cultural traits, practices and beliefs. Doing so could bring about greater uncertainty or confusion in your life. If you know who you are, where you have come from, have accepted your identity and believe that you are being true to yourself, it's that much easier to move forward and find meaning in your life.

As I showed earlier, this could also apply to your sexual orientation. You may deny your true feelings and conviction with regard to your gender identification because you are afraid of being judged or rejected by family or friends. However, if you are just presenting yourself as someone else to please everybody, then, eventually, your false sense of self will begin to take over and you won't know who you are anymore.

It's simple. How can you find meaning and purpose in your life if you don't know what your real needs, aspirations or dreams are? The stress of this confusion could eventually wear you down and lead you down the road to depression.

A LOW SELF-ESTEEM

In the previous chapter you saw how childhood insecurities can lead to a bad self-image and low self-esteem, which are factors that lead to the formation of feelings of anxiety and depression. These insecurities also create confusion and result in a loss of authenticity.

We also saw how, in adults, a low self-esteem can be due to bad living conditions such as poverty and unemployment, social exclusion or rejection. This low self-esteem leads to self-doubt and insecurity, which prompts even adults to seek attention, acceptance and respect. And, in turn, this opens them up to being easily influenced into doing things which they would normally not do, such as indulging in drugs, gangsterism and crime. Remember Melody's case study in this regard.

In turn, these actions can only alienate them further from themselves and they eventually become totally disconnected from the promptings of their authentic self and their conscience.

DYSFUNCTIONAL RELATIONSHIPS

Lies, pretence, fakeness and a false sense of self are all side-effects of inauthenticity, and none of these behaviours or attitudes are good for relationships. Once people find out that you are 'fake' and untrustworthy, you are likely to end up with major problems with social relationships and this can take you away from what is truly meaningful, such as family and good friends. It is far better to be honest with yourself and with others about who you are, where you came from and what your value system truly is. In other words, remain authentic.

CASE STUDY

Janet has had some horrible experiences on a well-known dating platform. Most of the problems relate to the guys not being who they pretended to be, either photoshopping their photos or lying about their lives to make themselves appear more successful and attractive. As a result, Janet no longer has any trust in this method of meeting new people and has also lost faith in men in general.

I think that all women (and men) would prefer their partners to be up front about themselves and not pretend, rather than being deceptive and trying to impress them.

You cannot have a meaningful relationship with someone who is pretending. Honesty shows integrity and authenticity. And even if the person does not look like a model, their vulnerability and authenticity can be very attractive – at least you will know that their feelings are genuine.

LIVING A LIE

Living a lie and being out of step with your authentic self – which comprises your ethics, true values and conscience – can cause cognitive dissonance, which can later lead to anxiety. Here we are speaking about misrepresenting yourself, creating a fake persona, wearing masks, pretence, and even hypocrisy and self-deception. It is also unlikely that you will ever find direction and meaning in your life if you are living a lie.

NOT BEING HONEST WITH YOURSELF

Most of us are guilty of this one: not always being honest with ourselves all the time. A simple case in question is when we feel social pressure to do something we are not really interested in. For instance, attending a family member's or friend's get-together. We find excuses for not attending these events and, if we try hard enough, we will always find one. These could be excuses such as 'we were not given enough notice' or 'the date is not suitable', or 'we have something important to do on that day', rather than admitting to ourselves that we simply didn't want to go to the event in the first place.

This is a very straightforward case of not being honest with oneself or with others and, as I said, I think many of us do this. But this shows how easy it is to become inauthentic.

HYPOCRISY: WEARING ONLY A MASK OF RESPECTABILITY

Sometimes people introduce their false self to the world by hiding behind a *mask of respectability*. An example of this would be a corrupt politician or activist who says that they are working for the good of 'the people' when, in fact, deep down, they are interested in their own advancement and they are acting with an ulterior motive and a hidden agenda. This is hypocrisy and, unfortunately, it is so common in our modern society.

CASE STUDY

Thomas is a well-known activist who belongs to a number of organisations which work for human and animal rights. He makes public statements about tolerance, compassion and understanding towards everyone. However, he gets very upset and nasty when some people challenge his ideas, opinions or beliefs or don't want to help with his fundraising.

This points to a contradiction between what Thomas believes and the way he behaves, which shows that he is not being authentic and is presenting a face to the world which does not match his true feelings and nature. He is hypocritical and fooling himself (and others) into believing that he's an altruistic, tolerant, loving person when, in fact, he is not.

FOOLING YOURSELF (SELF-DECEPTION)

This dishonesty with one's self can become worse and develop into what is called 'self-deception'. What starts out as a white lie or an attempt to impress others can become internalised and accepted by our psyches to the point where we don't even know that we are lying to ourselves. What this means is that we can actually convince or *fool ourselves* into believing that we are more influential, competent or altruistic than we really are in order to gain the respect and admiration we want. Our ego and our false sense of self won't allow us to accept our limitations, and this can lead to self-deception and even self-delusion, which is when we grow out of touch with reality.

CASE STUDY

John was overlooked for promotion as the result of a lack of performance, but he sees only other reasons for this failure, such as favouritism, victimisation and racism. He simply cannot see or accept that this situation was the result of this own behaviour and weak performance. In this case, John's self-deception is so bad that he remains incapable of seeing and accepting the truth, even if he is presented with the cold facts, such as the low marks allocated to him by the promotion board and the superior qualifications and experience of the other candidates.

SELF-DELUSION

But it can be even worse than this. For instance, a person who fools themself continuously into believing outlandish ideas about their being part of some conspiracy, some sort of victim or an unsung hero, which ideas are not true, is said to be self-delusional. This can be the result of strong emotions linked to their desperate need for their narrative to be true. In this case, their false sense of self is overriding their rational thinking. This is a bad case of a loss of authenticity.

CHAPTER 5
REGAINING YOUR AUTHENTICITY

Being authentic is not easy. It takes a lot of courage being yourself when you don't really fit in or agree with what is going on around you. Here I am speaking about peer pressure and also the demands of work roles and society's expectations.

Rediscovering your authenticity is even more difficult than being authentic, because it is not so much a process of learning but rather of unlearning all the bad habits associated with being inauthentic – such as pretence, lies and deception and accessing and expressing the best parts of yourself. To do so, you have to move through the veils of self-deception and be prepared to acknowledge the full truth about yourself. And this requires courage, as there may be real issues from the past that you will have to deal with, factors which have led to the creation of your false sense of self.

STEPS TO REGAINING YOUR AUTHENTICITY

You also have to be prepared to recultivate those authentic aspects and personality traits which were part of you originally before they got lost in inauthentic living. Here I am speaking about the four key factors highlighted by Drs Kernis and Goldman plus the extra one that I added, that of continuing on the path to conscious personal growth.

- Self-awareness (mindfulness), self-insight and self-knowledge
- An unbiased perspective (objectivity)
- Congruency
- The ability to maintain good relationships
- Conscious personal growth.

You may have to take active steps to rebuild these areas, such as counselling, coaching or personal growth courses. Authentic people are open and honest and therefore not afraid to seek help if they need it.

ACKNOWLEDGE YOUR AUTHENTICITY

Being authentic means being humble and not lying or exaggerating about your work, your life or your beliefs. Let go of the charade you present to the world to get attention and never be afraid of acknowledging the childlike innocence deep within you, that original state that was 'you' before the entanglements and stresses of the world and society strangled your authentic self. Be prepared to let go and enjoy yourself like a child whenever you can. Don't be ashamed of who you are. Your authenticity is more valuable than gold.

Healing may require you to share your story with trusted friends, counsellors or coaches and to be totally honest with them. Don't be afraid to show emotion, because an emotional release (catharsis) is an important part of becoming 'real' again.

Ask yourself the following questions:

- What are those aspects of my personality or make-up that I am ashamed of?
- What would I like to change about myself?
- What is stopping me from making these changes?

DEVELOP MORE SELF-AWARENESS (OR MINDFULNESS)

Self-awareness is extremely important for returning to authenticity. You need to stop the thoughtless actions that are so typical of inauthentic behaviour.

REFLECT ON YOURSELF AND YOUR ACTIONS

Try to remember yourself as you were before you lost your authenticity. Once you begin to remember who you were, you can again begin to trust your good intentions, your motives, the accuracy of what you truly feel, and your choices.

At this point, you need to do some self-examination. Start by recognising and accepting that you are behaving inauthentically and pinpoint the causes, such as a wearing masks (being fake) in order to gain acceptance, a promotion or that lucrative contract. Ambition or chasing after money and success is usually the most common cause in this case.

Second, you may be pretending to be someone you are not because you are afraid of being excluded or socially rejected. But by pretending you are only making things worse. If people won't accept you for who you really are, they are not 'your' people and not worth even worrying about.

So what if you had a poor childhood or have a bad background. Many of us have. You should not let it determine who you are or the values you espouse.

Ask yourself the following questions:

- What is it that is causing me conflict?
- Why do I feel this way?
- When did all this start? Is it something from my past?
- Why do I still feel the need to pretend, to deceive others or to behave in ways that inevitably make me feel uncomfortable?

A PRACTICAL EXPERIENCE OF MINDFULNESS

Mindfulness means being fully aware or conscious of what is happening around you and what you are thinking and doing *in the moment*, in the 'now'. Simply put, you are mindful when you are fully aware of your thoughts and the true feelings you have about a person or a situation and are able to pause for a moment, think and make conscious decisions. As a result, I could describe mindfulness as a blend of deep observation, mental clarity and efficiency.

HERE IS A SIMPLE EXERCISE TO INTRODUCE YOU TO MINDFULNESS

- Lift up your hands, look at them and move your fingers very slowly while repeating to yourself slowly, over and over, 'I'm alive!'
- Continue with this until, in one exhilarating moment, you actually become fully conscious of the fact that you are indeed alive.

This moment of pure self-awareness is one aspect of your true, authentic self, what it was like before you filled it up with all the concerns and masks of the false sense of self.

USE SUBLIMINAL COMMANDS

Here is a more advanced version of the previous exercise to help to put you in contact with your authentic self for a few seconds. It is based on a deeper form of self-realisation and helps you to access those subconscious parts of yourself where your authentic self is hidden.

First relax your body and try to quieten your mind. Now try this quick exercise to relax body and mind and induce mindfulness:

- Sit quietly and comfortably, close your eyes and begin to breathe to a count of one to five. Focus on nothing else but the counting (either aloud or in your mind).
- Breathe in 1,2,3,4,5, hold your breath 1,2,3,4, 5, breathe out 1,2,3,4,5, hold your breath 1,2,3,4,5, breathe in 1,2,3,4,5, and so on.

- Carry on with the counting and breathing until your mind is free of all thought, completely quiet, and you feel totally relaxed.
- Now open your mind and try to be fully aware, mindful and 'present' without actually thinking. With practise it can be done.

After you have reached this relaxed state of mind, lift up your hands in front of your face, look at your palms and move your fingers in front of you.

- Repeat the words, 'I'm alive' a few times.
- Now turn your hands towards your chest and focus on the area between your hands and your chest.
- Change the words to 'I am' and repeat them slowly over and over again a few times.
- Now change the words 'I am' to the word 'I'.
- Repeat the word 'I' a number of times, slowly and deliberately with intent.
- Surrender and abandon yourself to the full experience of what it is to be 'I.
- Carry on repeating 'I' with emotion until you suddenly take an unexpectedly quick, deep breath.

Don't be alarmed, this is normal. You have reached deep into your subconscious mind and had a momentary connection with your true *authentic self.* Practise this exercise whenever you feel lost or out of synchronicity with your true self.

TRY TO REDISCOVER YOUR TRUE IDENTITY

Perform a self-examination and try to remember your true identity, that which you were when you were a young person. What were your values, beliefs, dreams and aspirations at that time? Face up to the truths of who you are, where you came from, and the problems you have accumulated in your life. Be painfully honest with yourself. I know that this is not always easy, but doing so can set you free.

Ask yourself the following questions:

'WHO AM I?'

- What kind of person do I think I am?
- What do I feel about myself?
- Do I know what my values are?
- Do I know what makes me unique?

The problem is that some of your answers may come from your false sense of self, so you may have to go even deeper into your psyche to get to the truth. This will be done in later chapters.

ACCEPT YOURSELF

Accepting yourself is another important step towards returning to authenticity. This includes coming to terms with your past and working towards building and maintaining a positive self-image and a healthy self-esteem.

Many of us have had bad childhoods and past experiences. Look for the lessons in the pain of your past and learn from them.

Answer the following questions:

- Is there anything from my past that I'm ashamed of?
- Are there events in my past that I would rather not discuss with others?
- Am I covering up some pain from my past?

For example, if you now find yourself alone and depressed after a series of bad relationships, ask yourself if there was anything that you gained from those experiences? What did you learn from them?

For instance, you may have realised that being alone is not always a bad thing, as it gives you time to do self-reflection and gain self-insight. This means that you are more likely to stay authentic and in touch with yourself, as we can easily lose ourselves in busy lives of glamour or in shallow and meaningless relationships.

CHANGE YOUR ATTITUDE TO LIFE

YOUR PHILOSOPHY OF LIFE

Your attitude to life is affected by your *philosophy of life*. In other words, how you see life and what it means to you. This affects how you interpret your experiences and cope with life's day-to-day challenges. But it can also be a factor contributing to your anxiety and it can lead to negative self-talk. However, changing your attitude to life can also help you to return to authenticity.

LIFE METAPHORS

An easy way of identifying your approach to or philosophy of life is the *metaphor* you choose to use for your view of life. In this case, the metaphor would be a word-symbol with a deeper meaning that represents your approach to life and the way you view it. This can either be a positive, uplifting view of life or a negative, unhelpful one.

For example:

If you think of *life as a battle*, you could begin to see other people as enemies and opportunities as threats. No wonder you experience anxiety!

However, the return of your authenticity will ground you and you can change your metaphor of life to one of life *being a classroom*, in which you learn and grow. And you may begin to see challenges as lessons or opportunities to learn new skills. In a classroom situation we are all learning and often don't have all the answers to the questions that are being put to us. All that is needed is that we be willing to learn and keep our minds open to new information that will improve our understanding of life.

THE ANALOGY OF A COMPUTER GAME

A reasonable person will accept that life is naturally full of challenges which we all have to face and overcome to move to the next level, almost like a computer game. In fact, a computer game would also make an interesting metaphor for life. Perhaps if you don't like the idea of a classroom, you could accept the challenges of life as being similar to an online game and take that on as your new metaphor.

This is where your rational (authentic) self comes into play.

It is unfortunately a fact of life that you will be continually faced with situations which affect you and threaten your peace of mind. However, you now have a new avatar which is more powerful than the last one and perhaps you will be more successful this time round.

So ask yourself what you truly want out of life. What has meaning for you? Start thinking more deeply about what is meaningful and purposeful to you. Consider the following questions:

- What's it about life that makes me anxious?
- Is it my philosophy of life? How do I view life?
- What does life mean to me?
- What is my own metaphor for life?

TAKE BACK YOUR VALUE SYSTEM

Re-evaluate what you are prepared to do, and what you are not, when it comes to moral and ethical issues.

Begin by taking an independent stand on those issues that really matter to you. Sticking to your values does not mean arguing with any person who expresses a different opinion, because, ethically, we are all entitled to our own opinion; but it does mean simply staying true to your own heartfelt values and beliefs. For example: If a group discussion is radical or spewing prejudice, judgements or hatred towards others, I can assure you that challenging those present will not help. People don't change that easily, at least not until something radical happens in their lives to show them the errors or unreasonableness of their thinking. In such circumstances, it's best to simply walk away and join another conversation group.

However, it is important that you know how and where you stand on some important issues.

Ask yourself the following questions:

- How do I feel about politics?
- How do I feel about religion
- How do I feel about the LGBTQIA+ community?

There are no right or wrong answers here. The idea is to put you in touch with your real feelings on controversial subjects. If an answer implies judgement, ask yourself whether there is something that happened in your past which makes you feel this way about this issue. An authentic person is not biased; on the contrary, they are tolerant, reasonable and open to considering all opinions, without necessarily agreeing with them. As I have said, it is not a question of having to say something to please others; its sufficient just to know what your own true, sincere and authentic feelings on a matter are.

LEARN TO THINK AND ACT FOR YOURSELF

When you have to make decisions that will affect you, always ask yourself if this is what you truly want to do or just someone else's idea. If you are being pressurised by someone else, or caught off guard and feel you have to make this decision, you will feel uncomfortable and anxious. Try to remember what the real issues are, who you truly are inside, and act authentically according to your core values and beliefs.

Ask yourself the following questions:

- Is what I believe based on my true convictions and the facts that I have researched?
- Am I sure that my ideas are my own and not influenced by what others want me to think?
- Am I trying to please others by adopting this position or do I really feel this way?

Here are some tips in this regard:

- Use your feelings. Being uncomfortable in a situation is a good sign of being out of synchronicity with your true authentic self. What is it that you are thinking of doing that is in conflict with your values and beliefs?
- Keep in touch with your conscience. Your conscience is the promptings of your authentic self. If you believe that you will feel guilty about what you are doing, then you know that it is not in alignment with your true values and beliefs.
- Try to be aware of the underlying motives and issues of others, and also of the real implications and consequences of what will happen before you make decisions. This means remaining mindful at all times.
- Also learn to think logically according to your own beliefs and convictions. How to think independently and critically is covered in my latest book *Critical thinking*.

REDISCOVERING YOUR MEANING AND PURPOSE

One of the first and most important steps in returning to authenticity is to rediscover your meaning and purpose in life. This is also essential to dealing with feelings of depression. Seeing meaning in your life and having a purpose will give you hope and something to strive (and live) for if you are caught up in feelings of depression.

Here is a series of questions that will help you with this task.

WHAT DO YOU REALLY WANT FROM LIFE?

- **Identify the things you care about**

Your life's purpose is usually related to your contribution to society or the world in general and is not really about you as a person. People such as activists have a cause for which they are ready to work and will persist even if it is difficult doing so. I am not saying that everyone should be involved in human and animal rights or social or environmental activism, but they are an example of people having a definite goal and purpose and being involved in something bigger than themselves.

It's all about knowing yourself and working for your ideals as part of being authentic. This idea of selflessly working for others could also form part of your plan for dealing with the loss of meaning that usually accompanies feelings of depression. It could entail, for instance, applying your skills and contributing to a worthy cause in a way that matters to you. So, identify what you care about and consider getting involved in an NGO which works with those matters. It can be lay counselling, the upliftment of poor communities, fundraising for charities, or supporting or performing animal care. The idea is to find meaning and purpose in your life in order to return to authenticity.

- **Reflect on what matters most in your life**

Everyone has values, ideals and dreams that they would like to fulfil. Consider your dreams and aspirations, these could be things that you have always wanted to do with your life (your 'bucket list'), whether it is to travel or do something creative such as art, music or writing. Start thinking about something that you may have missed in your life, the idea of which excites you. Everyone needs a creative outlet and an over-taxing workload without any other interest or activity to balance it out can lead to burnout and other emotional problems. Try to find balance in your life, which is also an aspect of authenticity.

- **Prioritise your values**

People able to regain their authenticity act according to their value system. Safeguarding values such as loyalty, honesty, integrity, diligence, dependability, courage, empathy and compassion will be useful when trying to identify your ultimate purpose in life. You have been given these personality attributes for a reason, and during self-actualisation you are able to express them fully.

- **Recognise your strengths and talents**

We all have strengths and skills that we've developed over our lifetime. These now make up part of our unique personalities. And now that you have decided to use this book as a guide back to the path of personal growth, identify those traits and strengths that are linked to your authenticity, as this will help you to progress further along your chosen path.

Here I am referring to rational and emotional skills such as mindfulness, emotional intelligence, congruency, logical thinking, flexibility, objectivity and resilience – you will need to embrace them more fully. Recovering these strengths and talents in your life and being able to apply them will boost your self-esteem and open up the path to your self-actualisation through service.

Perhaps with all the absent fathers in today's societies, just being a good mother and focusing on your children can give you the direction and purpose you seek. Many women have come from the brink of despair by being prepared to sacrifice their own needs (sometimes their whole lives) for the sake of their children.

CASE STUDY

Pat was a young mother whose husband left her when the children were young. Her ex-husband simply wanted to put the children into an orphanage, and it was left to her alone to defend, protect, reassure and guide her four small boys through adolescence and into adulthood. Their father did not play a role in their lives at all. Pat never got into an intimate relationship again; instead, she gave up her social life and independence and lived in poverty with her children. But this was a sacrifice she was prepared to make. Pat was very proud of the way her children had turned out to be good people, but she died at an early age soon after she held her first grandchild. But she has never been forgotten by her children and is remembered for her strength in fighting the system and keeping the family together in dire circumstances. This woman was my mother, and this is a true story.

She provides an example of how a life of sacrifice and suffering had almost a divine purpose. From her I learnt the power of faith and inner strength, which has served me well in my own difficult situations.

So, let's all try to learn from this story and cultivate positive aspects such as faith, hope, love and charity – plus gratitude for what we have. Your life could very well have been different if someone hadn't carried you at some time along the way.

- **Try volunteering**

I have already mentioned volunteering at NGOs and community centres to make a meaningful difference in the world. There is nothing quite like the smile of gratitude on the face of a child who can never repay your help or support to make one realise that life doesn't revolve around one, but rather it involves humanity as a whole.

However, make sure that any organisation you join is the right 'fit' for you, otherwise you could end up experiencing anxiety again.

- **Aim for self-actualisation**

Imagine your best possible self and strive to be that. Conscious steps towards personal growth will also give you purpose. This means doing courses or attending talks and lectures all designed to help you develop those natural attributes, skills and strengths that you possess (perhaps without even realising it). Learning never stops, and even if you are in your 60s or 70s, if you are prepared to make the effort, you can still return to authenticity and achieve self-actualisation.

- **Emulate people you admire**

Sometimes the people we admire most in life give us a clue as to how we might want to contribute to a better world ourselves. If you are religious, read about the lives of the saints and martyrs and how they coped with horrendous circumstances. If you are not, consider the lives of civil-rights leaders or rights activists of various shades. Following the lessons of these moral leaders can only help you to regain your own self-actualisation.

CHAPTER 6

WHAT ARE ANXIETY AND DEPRESSION?

There are many ways of treating anxiety and depression, but recent studies have shown a link between a return to authenticity and the management of these two states of mind, and this forms the focus for this book. Let's have a quick look at their characteristics, starting with anxiety.

ANXIETY

Anxiety is a very unpleasant state of tension which relates to an overpowering fear or worry of some situation or event that you have to face in the future. The problem is that, if you do not face and deal with this fear or threat, over time the anxiety will eat away at your energy and you may start down that dark road to depression.

In this book we examine in-depth one of the reasons for anxiety, namely a loss of authenticity and the inner conflict that it produces. This means that we know we are living a lie, a double life of pretence, and eventually we will not know who we truly are. Nor will we know what is important for us to establish or focus on our meaning and purpose in this life, and what we need to do to ensure our happiness and fulfilment, as we have become so used to pretending to be someone else.

EXISTENTIAL ANXIETY

Even highly intelligent and authentic people could be subject to what is called *existential anxiety*, which is a feeling of dread or apprehension that comes from thinking about our mortality and the meaning of life and death. It's the realisation that life is uncertain. We all have to accept that existential anxiety is a normal part of life, because few of us have the confidence to face life without seeing its clear purpose or meaning. This is why it is so important to find that meaning while on the road to your return to authenticity.

DEPRESSION

Depression is a mood disorder that includes feelings of sadness and loss of interest. It is linked to both prolonged anxiety and many other mental disorders and factors, some of which I have already mentioned in chapter three. Depression usually occurs at the end of a long road of trying to cope with disappointment, humiliation, betrayal, resentment or other negative emotions. And the final feeling is one of having given up and then entering a deep, dark place where you just want to be left alone.

This negative state of mind will affect all areas of your life: your work, home, personal relationships and social life. And you may experience problems with pursuing normal day-to-day activities as your energy levels are very low. You feel as if you are at the lowest point in your life and you simply don't care anymore.

It is not something that you can just 'snap out of', though. This is because real chemical changes that have taken place in the brain en route to becoming depressed. In severe cases, depression can lead to a nadir of suicidal thoughts.

PRACTICAL TIPS TO HELP WITH ANXIETY AND THE FEELINGS ASSOCIATED WITH DEPRESSION

Anyone experiencing anxiety will often second-guess themselves and wonder if they have actually paid all the bills and dealt with all their important correspondence. While you are still on the road to authenticity, you could become a bit scatter-brained as a result of all the inner conflicts and tensions that affect your thinking processes. It is well known that it is easy to overlook something when you are constantly preoccupied with your own thoughts.

You will find that you are able to cope better with anxiety if you develop a number of little strategies or 'crutches' which will help you in practical ways.

Here are a number of techniques which I have learnt over the years that have helped me cope with anxiety and depression:

BACK UP YOUR FILING SYSTEM.
CHECK AND DOUBLE-CHECK EVERYTHING

One factor that feeds my own anxiety is private-sector and government incompetence. There is nothing that makes me more anxious than when I have to deal with bureaucratic systems that don't work properly or poorly trained consultants who cannot think for themselves or who make decisions without consulting the handbook. Human beings make mistakes, but when mistakes become institutionalised, for me, it's a great source of worry and irritation.

Always compensate for the human factor by making sure you have all your ducks in a row and that you have all the correct supporting documentation.

LET ME SHARE SOME REAL-LIFE EXAMPLES WITH YOU

In the old days we used to have cheque books linked to our bank accounts and wrote cheques to pay bills. I cannot tell you how many times these cheques saved my bacon. For instance, it was a favourite pastime of some companies to tell you that an account hadn't been paid, and it was a very gratifying feeling to be able to wave a bank-stamped and cashed cheque in the face of a creditor. Unfortunately, cheques are no longer legal tender and we now have to make sure that we keep some sort of *acknowledgement of receipt*. Insist on such a receipt whenever you send important documents.

In another case, I had to send a second batch of completed forms when the first batch was mysteriously 'lost'. This happens very easily. To cover yourself against such incidents, keep copies of important documents that you send to different departments, as you never know when they will become 'misplaced'. Use a courier service, if you can, as they are more reliable than the post office (in this country, anyway).

Today, most transactions are implemented either by online banking or by email in the case of correspondence. All I can say to you is to first check, double-check and even triple-check that you have sent the documents to the correct email address (it is best to phone beforehand to verify). And always ensure that you have received an acknowledgement of a payment or for any documents emailed. And if not, ask for a confirmation and don't let up until your get a reply.

It is also a good idea to make hard copies of important correspondence by scanning the original and keeping a paper filing system as a back-up. Your computer could crash and you could lose your data or you could struggle to find and recover the relevant computer file later on.

For instance, I have had an experience where a consultant in a business institution didn't inform her co-worker in the same office about what she had already done on my case, and I had to resend all the emails and scans I had on record to prove that the documents had already been forwarded to her colleague. Having redundancy built into your filing system when it comes to your business records will reduce your anxiety, as you know that you have everything on computer in addition to hard copies in your filing system.

WATCH OUT FOR SPAM AND SCAMS

The internet has unfortunately opened up a Pandora's box of spam and scams, and this is another great source of anxiety to many of us. There is a lot of spam out there and an untold number of scams daily out there. You therefore need to know how to identify scams and how to deal with them, otherwise your anxiety will only get worse.

WHAT IS SPAM?

Phone, email or SMS spam can be broadly categorised as any phone call, email or SMS message you didn't expect or ask for. Usually, a person or business is calling or sending you an unsolicited newsletter, email or SMS to try to manipulate you into buying their product. It can be very irritating to get dozens of these phone calls, emails, Whatsapps or SMSs during the day, and these will only serve to raise your anxiety level.

There are a number of ways in which you can handle this:

You can block phone calls and WhatsApp's from unknown numbers on your smartphone (get someone to help you if you are not sure how). In the case of emails, newsletters or advertisements, there is normally an 'unsubscribe' button or link at the top or the bottom of the page. Simply on this click this link and wait for an acknowledgement that you have been removed from their lists (or 'unsubscribed').

On your computer, unwanted spam can easily be flagged and blocked. MS Outlook can be programmed to automatically mark an email address as spam and send it to your trash or spam file. To do so, right-click on the email, select 'Junk' and then select 'Block Sender'.

You can program your MS Outlook to be less tolerant of any unwanted emails using the junk email options. In this case, select 'Junk' and then 'Junk email options' on the menu and change the spam-spotting level from 'low' to 'high', and click OK.

SCAMS

Scam emails or cellphone calls or messages are designed to fool unsuspecting people into giving out bank details or downloading malware or dangerous attachments, which can lead to you losing a lot of money. No one is immune: we all receive these scam messages. Scammers send out thousands of them at any one time. And they need only a few people to fall prey to their insidious game for them to be successful. I have noted that scammers specifically target older people who are often not that computer-savvy.

It's a sad indictment on our society that scammers would especially target the elderly and vulnerable, taking away from the little income from pensions and grants that they depend upon.

Knowing that they can be scammed at any time can cause a vulnerable person extreme anxiety and so they have to find ways of protecting themself and stopping the scammers' game.

The first thing to do is set all your online accounts and social media platforms for two-factor authentication (2FA). This means that the platform you are attempting to access or log in to will check with you twice before allowing you in. This normally involves you having to provide the usual password together with some kind of code or one-time password (OTP) or your pressing a verification link that pops up on the screen of your computer or smartphone.

If a scam artist somehow bypasses your password, with 2FA the chances of their having access to your phone or computer are low, because they do not have your phone in their hands.

TWO-STEP VERIFICATION

- Open your Google account.
- In the navigation panel, select **'Security'**.
- Under 'Signing into Google', select **2-Step Verification** and then **'Get started'**.
- Follow the on-screen steps.

TYPES OF SCAMS

There are many different scams out there, such as advertising and marketing scams, a false package delivery scam, money scams (a free offer or a lucky winner scam), scam emails which look as if they come from your bank or a government department, the love-trap scams, scams designed to scare you into giving up your banking information (your account has supposedly been compromised), threatening scams (they pretend to have hacked your account or computer and demand money), plus attachments infected with ransomware. (Ransomware is malicious software that locks and encrypts a victim's data, files, devices or systems, rendering them inaccessible and unusable until the attacker receives a ransom payment.) Scammers can even now hack into your email system and give their fraudulent banking details when you have to make an EFT payment to someone else. Another threat and source of anxiety is the practice of phishing. It is a common type of cyber-attack that targets individuals through email, text messages, phone calls and other forms of communication. A phishing attack aims to trick the recipient into falling for the attacker's desired action, such as revealing financial information, system login credentials or other sensitive information.

Fundamentally, these threats exploit human psychology rather than technical vulnerabilities.

More information on these cyberscams and how to spot and stop them is a huge section on its own and falls outside the scope of this book. However, these steps can be found in my latest publication *Critical thinking*. As I have stated, just knowing that these scammers are out there will make any person nervous and this only adds to their anxiety.

ORGANISE EFFECTIVELY

A disorganised office or study can only cause you more anxiety as you struggle to remember where you put something or you tend to forget important dates and deadlines.

We all have loads of business correspondence, accounts and bills to pay and this can be very confusing and daunting if everything is just kept loosely on your desk or a table at home. We also forget easily when it is stored only on a computer and not everyone is so computer savvy as to set up reminders.

I may be a bit old-fashioned in this regard, but, as I said, I have found it useful to get a few small filing cabinets with files and sub-files and to store copies of all my correspondence in these files in addition to storing them on my computer. Think of the in- and out-trays, and also the 'pending' trays, we used to use in the 'old' days. They seem simple and outmoded but they are actually still an easy way of organising things and they certainly continue to reduce my anxiety.

To sum up, do not depend only on your computer records. My actual correspondence is still conducted online using the internet, but I have found this duplicate hard-copy system to be more tangible and less stressful, because I can open the folder that I am busy with and have all the necessary documents inside them. And I do not have to search for each of them on my computer. Trying to find old correspondence on a computer can sometimes be difficult and cause anxiety, especially if you can't remember where you stored it.

If something pops up unexpectedly that also needs your attention, just stick a Post-it on your computer with the details written on it so that you won't forget to attend to it.

FLEXIBILITY

Remember that with authenticity comes reasonableness. Some-times people set themselves unreasonable time frames, trying to get everything done in one day. This puts enormous pressure on them and can lead to stress and anxiety when something unex-pected happens to delay the work.

It is also important not to worry about the things going on around you which you can't control. Just do the best you can.

CHIP AWAY AT BIG PROJECTS

In other words, you need to become more flexible, not rigidly dogmatic about getting everything done immediately. Rather *chip away* consistently at a large project, one day at a time, giving your-self time in between to rest and adjust to the work.

CASE STUDY

Tony is an anxiety sufferer and every year when it comes to doing his tax return he becomes stressed out and anxious as it is quite a daunting task for him. However, over the years, Tony has learnt a few tricks (coping mechanisms) which help him to manage his anxiety when having to deal with large projects like this. He opens a file and sets himself the goal to do a page or two each day. Working like this, it takes him a few weeks to complete his tax return, but he can handle this bit-by-bit approach; and as long as he keeps moving forward, he is satisfied.

Eventually, he completes the complex tax return, but just not in the unreasonable time frame that he used to set for himself.

PRIORITISE

There is a popular saying which goes like this: 'Don't sweat the small stuff.' I have found it to be particularly helpful. One way of preventing yourself sweating the small stuff is to get yourself a wall or desk calendar, one of those with the large blocks in which you can write down important messages. Write all the due dates of your appointments, projects and business dealings on the calendar and use this for your planning. Visual aids like this will reduce the anxiety you may experience if you can't remember, as you can immediately and clearly see all the important meetings, dates and times on the calendar on the wall or desktop in front of you.

DO BETTER TIME MANAGEMENT

Sometimes being late can cause you to rush and increase your anxiety level. Rather commit to leaving early and getting to your destination at least 15 minutes before the time. This relieves the pressure and also helps you to develop a healthy self-discipline. If you have an important online or face-to-face presentation coming up, make sure that you prepare, giving yourself plenty of time, so that you feel confident about it and don't feel nervous or anxious.

ONLINE SHOPPING

Better time management may include your doing more online shopping, especially if the stores are far away from you. The money you save on fuel will cover any extra expenses you may incur with having your groceries delivered.

Many people today, especially the elderly, are turning to online shopping and delivery as a way of avoiding driving long distances and reducing the stress of going out alone. Of course, the only problem is that you have to be able to work on the internet or on a smartphone and this can be daunting for some people, especially the elderly. Here, young people can provide a great service by helping their aged parents or relatives with this kind of online work.

CHAPTER 7
A RATIONAL (CBT) APPROACH TO DEALING WITH ANXIETY AND DEPRESSION

GETTING PROFESSIONAL HELP

Sometimes you may be far down the road to experiencing anxiety or depression and you can't see the way back to authenticity. If you are already at this point, you will need professional help. You can't become authentic or self-actualise yourself if you are caught up in the hurricane of emotions I wrote about earlier. Rest assured, though, that there is no shame in going for medical or psychiatric treatment. The world is not what it used to be. *Undiagnosed mental illness* is one of the biggest problems we face in society today and I can only advise you to seek professional help first and then look at regaining your authenticity once you have become stabilised. In fact, if you are in a chronic state of anxiety or depression, it is unlikely that you will ever be able to self-actualise until you have dealt with these conditions effectively. So your first step should be to consult a professional.

CONSULT A PROFESSIONAL

- Seek guidance and advice from a mental health professional such as a psychiatrist or a psychotherapist to obtain a proper diagnosis and treatment plan.
- There is no shame in taking medication for anxiety and depression, as trying to cope on your own, even with the eventual goal of returning to authenticity, could take a long time. In fact, in severe cases, it may be a lifelong struggle.

TREATMENT DURATION

- Depending on the severity of your symptoms, medical treatment may take several weeks, months or even years before you feel an improvement in your condition.

SELF-HELP TECHNIQUES

In this book I use a rational (cognitive) approach which involves looking at the negative self-talk, irrational beliefs and self-destructive thoughts which may be creating or sustaining your negative feelings and worsening your condition. Later on, I guide you in formulating a plan comprising action steps and changes to your lifestyle which may also help you.

If you apply yourself, you may be able to return to authenticity by using these self-help techniques. However, as mentioned above, this could take a long time.

The techniques have been framed in the form of case studies, which makes them more accessible and also makes it easier to see the steps and processes in action. In each case, you should substitute your own story for the plots of the case studies and tackle the steps one at a time.

Make sure that you remain congruent and stable throughout. If you feel distressed and that you are losing control, see a counsellor or a therapist, as it may be that your situation is worse than you thought. As I wrote earlier, these self-help techniques are not meant to cure anxiety disorders or clinical depression, which need specialist intervention and medication. These rational steps should be considered only as an aid to helping you cope better with the negative emotions and thoughts associated with these conditions.

To begin, I will first show you how to identify the emotions that are affecting you. Some of them may already be active at a subliminal level and you may have to 'flush them out', so to speak.

Second, I will help you to identify the negative self-talk associated with these emotions. By challenging and refuting these ideas, you may be able to dismantle the framework that is sustaining the emotions and gain some relief.

Finally, I will demonstrate how to reformulate your ideas and restructure your thinking and actions to bring them back in line with your authentic self. This is not easy, as you have to be willing to make the necessary mental and emotional shifts.

DEALING WITH EMOTIONS

Let's begin by dealing first with your emotions because the rational tools you need to use will not work if you are still caught up in powerful emotions and are unable to think clearly.

Both anxiety and depression could include emotions such as anger and resentment. Repressed emotions such as these create terrible tensions that, if left untreated, could place you on the road to depression. These can include anger and resentment; feelings of uselessness and worthlessness, and guilt and self-blame. Each of these is considered below.

ANGER AND RESENTMENT

Anger is not necessarily a bad emotion. It can be motivating and provide you with the energy to take action and get out of a toxic situation. In other words, if directed wisely, anger can be positive. The problem arises when it's allowed to fester over many months or years and it transforms into *resentment*, which is a destructive emotion that can lead you down the wrong path.

Let's have a look at a real-life case study of the motivating power of anger. Obviously names have been changed in the interests of confidentiality.

CASE STUDY

Catherine was stuck in a rut at work and was feeling depressed. She then decided that she wanted to study to improve her position and her chances of promotion. The company had a policy of helping workers to study further with bursaries and so Catherine applied for one of these help schemes.

However, the company declined her application, saying that they did not think that she had the potential to obtain the degree she wanted. This infuriated Catherine, who directed her anger wisely and immediately signed up for the degree part time at her own expense. Her positive self-talk, if put into words, would be 'I will show what I can do'. This motivated her to continue her studies until she eventually obtained her PhD.

This reminds me of something Frank Sinatra once said: 'Massive success is the best Revenge.' In other words, when someone puts you down, enjoy the satisfaction of showing them how very wrong they were.

Unfortunately, if not directed or treated correctly, anger can turn into a toxic form of resentment and poison every aspect of your life.

Have a look at the following case study in which a rational process of evaluation, careful consideration of the costs and benefits of hanging on to negative emotions and conscious decision-making is followed to try to release these emotions. If you are also troubled by such emotions, try to apply these techniques to your own situation.

CASE STUDY

Joan is a middle-aged lady whose husband left for a younger woman some years ago.

For many years she was filled with anger, which spilt over into her daily life and affected all her relationships. She was often avoided by her colleagues and old friends, who said she had become irritable, negative and toxic. This social judgement and isolation only made things worse for her, as it led to her becoming anxious and having negative feelings that pointed to depression.

When we look at the long-term effects on her life, though, we see an even sadder story. Joan stopped going out altogether and did not trust men at all. The repressed anger and resentment had stopped her from having a normal working and social life. The way she felt towards men also limited her chances of ever finding love again.

Joan read widely about her condition and decided to help herself by trying a rational (CBT) approach to emotional healing. She hoped that by exploring new perspectives and different points of view on her situation she would reach a better understanding of her situation and an acceptance of what had happened. She would also be able to let go and return to being the authentic young woman she knew she used to be.

In this section I use Joan's case study as a baseline and share four steps you can take as a rational approach to helping you deal with toxic emotions such as anger and resentment in order to put you back on the road to authentic living. In this case, these steps have been reformulated to fit a self-help approach.

THESE ARE THE FOUR STEPS JOAN USED.
Try to apply them to your own unresolved emotions:

Step 1: Identify your unresolved emotions.
Step 2: Try to unlock these emotions (catharsis).
Step 3: Rationally consider the effects of these emotions.
Step 4: Consciously decide to let them go.

STEP 1: IDENTIFY YOUR UNRESOLVED EMOTIONS

Joan struggled to recall all the details of the circumstances that led to her anger and resentment, because the incident had been very painful for her. However, eventually, she was able to acknowledge and identify her emotions: anger, resentment, bitterness and, finally, humiliation – an emotion that she had not recognised at the time.

STEP 2: TRY TO UNLOCK THESE EMOTIONS (CATHARSIS)

We know that powerful emotions can affect our thinking. In this case, catharsis means being able to release blocked or repressed emotions so as to allow your mind to settle down into a level of rational thinking in which you can review and evaluate your situation with a reasonable degree of objectivity. This enables you to gain new insights into an incident and an unbiased level of understanding that you would normally not gain if you were still very distressed.

This process of catharsis normally occurs as spontaneous crying or sobbing when you start to remember the pain of the event or incident and your metaphorical emotional 'wound' is unwrapped and exposed. If you are able to channel this emotional upset in a positive way, it can be very therapeutic.

Catharsis is normally encouraged during counselling, at which time you should ideally have someone there to support you. In Joan's case, she was lucky to have a sympathetic family member with her. Recalling the events which led to her husband's infidelity and their divorce had the desired effect of 'opening the valve' and releasing the emotions. As a result, she was able to start weeping softly, which is normal and to be encouraged during this part of the process. She felt a little better after her good cry and was ready for the next step in the process.

STEP 3: RATIONALLY CONSIDER THE EFFECTS OF THESE EMOTIONS

Anger and resentment are two of the most powerful emotions associated with anxiety and depression and which can cause the most damage to your health and well-being. However, let's continue with the case study and Joan's rational processing and see how you could apply this to yourself.

In this case, Joan weighed up the costs versus the benefits of her hanging on to her repressed emotions for such a long time. She considered the fact that it had been years since he had left and she could not understand why she was still angry, bitter and resentful towards him. She began rationally to question herself to discover the reason why this had been the case and why she had allowed these emotions to take control of her life.

Logically, there was no chance of a reconciliation as her ex-husband had married again and moved on. There was also no possible motive linked to revenge or making him feel guilty, as there had been no further contact between them.

Following this line of reasoning, Joan eventually came to the conclusion that, after the initial shock, she had become very angry. She also realised that this anger had given her the energy and the resolve to cope with the divorce; so, at the time, her anger had been necessary and useful to help to give her back some sort of control over her life.

COMMENT

This is quite understandable and normal under these circumstances. The problem really presents itself when one hangs on to the anger for too long and it crystallises into resentment, which can poison one's entire life. However, the question remained: Why did Joan still hang on to this anger and resentment for years after the divorce?

In hindsight, Joan recalls that she did not receive any form of counselling and this anger was therefore unresolved and must have carried on simmering. Over time it had therefore become resentment, probably sustained by her self-talk from the time of the break-up. She recalls that her thoughts at the time were very negative: the fact that she could never forgive him. And it was probably this thought that kept her resentment alive and ongoing. Without any way of dealing with her emotions after the break-up, they had festered until they became toxic.

Having now come to some sort of an understanding about why she couldn't let go of them, she now began to consider what these toxic emotions had cost her in respect of her family, work and social life. Fortunately, she was able to remember what had happened a few months after the break-up:

At first, her family and friends had rallied to help and support her, but due to her negativity and unwillingness to talk about it, they eventually gave up. This meant that both her family and her social relationships were now strained.

Second, she recalls how her work colleagues also supported her in the beginning, but eventually began to avoid her both at work and socially. However, in hindsight, Joan could now see more clearly the reasons for this avoidance behaviour: she had been pushing them away with her negative thinking and constant complaining. Apart from these consequences, her health was also suffering, as her blood pressure was raised and she was having frequent headaches and experiencing body pains, which were also affecting her ability to work.

Armed with these new insights, Joan could see that she was responsible for their behaviour towards her as well as her own lack of a social life, due to her mistrust of men. (Being honest with oneself and taking responsibility in this way always helps one to regain some authenticity and self-esteem.)

THE TURNING POINT

It was during this time of self-evaluation that Joan had a moment of insight – you could say it was the *turning point* in her rational processing. She now realised that she had been indirectly allowing her ex-husband's actions to control her life and that she had labelled herself as a victim, carrying all the negativity that goes with a victim complex.

COMMENT

People with a victim complex feel as though bad things keep happening to them and that everyone – even their family and friends, and also people in the world in general – is conspiring against them. This is a very unpleasant and dangerous state of mind.

It could be seen as a form of depression in which you blame others for your misfortunes and won't accept responsibility for your own mistakes. There may be some benefits which keep this state of mind going, such as receiving sympathy or attention for what happened to you, but the victim complex is one of the signposts on the way to depression.

THOSE WITH A VICTIM MENTALITY HOLD THREE BELIEFS:

- Bad things have happened in the past and will continue to happen to me.
- Others are to blame for my misfortune.
- There is no point in trying to bring about change because it will not work.

The problem is that developing a victim complex can easily lead to resentment and a loss of authenticity, as you can't see your own role and responsibilities in your situation and you will continually blame others for what goes wrong in your life. This means that you are no longer in touch with your true self, which is the rational, reasonable, objective and unbiased part of yourself.

To return to Joan's case study: she finally also realised that she had lost her connection to her authentic self, because she had to continually wear masks to try to act normally and to cover up her feelings of resentment and victimhood.

STEP 4: CONSCIOUSLY DECIDE TO LET THEM GO

Now reasoning with a new clarity and logic, Joan was able to come to the conclusion that there was simply no longer any benefit in hanging on to this resentment and that the cost of this and her victim complex were simply too high. She was estranged from her family and friends, she had no social life, and her health and work were suffering. She wanted her authenticity, her life and her health returned to her.

Joan was now ready to make a conscious decision that it was time to let go of her ex-husband and his actions, and also of her negative emotions. However, it was important for her to know that she was not releasing them because he had been justified in any way for what he did. No, *she was doing it for herself*, for her own peace of mind and, ultimately, for her own emotional and physical health.

After all these months, the negative feelings and self-talk had filtered through into her subconscious mind. But after reading up on different approaches, Joan decided to try *affirmations* to counter the effects of her negative feelings and self-talk. Affirmations are positive self-statements which, if properly internalised and taken up by our subconscious mind, can help to change the negative feelings and the subliminal self-talk that remain there.

Our knowledge about the effectiveness of affirmations is based on the work of the psychiatrist, Milton Eriksen, who believed that emotionally charged words have the power to affect our subconscious minds and bring about change to any negative self-beliefs we have stored there. In other words, if you decide to use affirmations, you will have to put real emotion and conviction into what you say and really mean it. Affirmations also work better when you say them out loud and are mindful and self-aware. This can usually be brought about by looking at yourself in a mirror: seeing your own image brings about a moment of self-realisation which helps to sustain mindfulness.

As a result, the first thing Joan did was to stand in front of her mirror and say to herself that she wanted to be whole and authentic again. She then made a conscious decision that this was the time and that the reasons are her own, for her own sake, to allow herself to heal and to move on with her life. She decided that she was no longer going to allow her ex-husband's actions to control her, as this is what was indirectly happening.

Joan also decided to perform a little ritual where she wrote down the reasons for her anger, resentment and humiliation on a piece of paper, made a new commitment to heal and be whole again and then tore it up in front of the mirror.

At the same time, she affirmed the following statements out loud, filled with emotion and intent:

> 'I am letting go of this anger and resentment.'
> 'I will no longer allow them to control me.'
> 'I am whole again.'
> 'I am authentic and real.'

Joan used these affirmations a few times each day until she began to feel stronger and less anxious. She had succeeded in taking back her personal power and authenticity.

COMMENT

If you are a spiritual or a religious person, you can also consider this last process as an act of forgiveness, if you wish to.

FEELINGS OF USELESSNESS AND WORTHLESSNESS

Let's continue with this process of self-healing using the rational method by linking it to a different case study, this time one which exposes the feelings of uselessness and worthlessness which are usually associated with depression. In this case, I have included a counsellor in the process, because depression is a dangerous state of mind which usually requires a qualified therapist to deal with it. However, you may be able to apply some of the steps and techniques to yourself – although, in the case of such powerful emotions, I would certainly recommend that someone be there to support you.

CASE STUDY

Carol was in a relationship with a man for about a year. In the beginning he was charming and considerate, but as time went on he became moody and demanding. She recalled that her friends had warned her against him, saying that he was a narcissist, but she was lonely and needy and went blindly into the relationship. Eventually, he became downright emotionally abusive and accused her of being useless and worthless as a girlfriend. This broke Carol's spirit and alienated her from both her family and friends and her own sense of authenticity. She could feel herself slipping into depression, but she did not have the strength to break free from the relationship because of his threats.

However, when she found him with another woman, that was the catalyst she needed.She became so angry that she threw his clothes out of the flat which she was renting and broke off the relationship. In this case, her anger gave her strength and energy to rid herself of this toxic relationship.

Soon after this episode, Carol saw a counsellor, who helped her to follow a CBT (rational) approach to rebuilding her shattered self-esteem, regain her authenticity and heal emotionally. As before, this approach incorporates the same four steps:

Step 1: Identify your unresolved emotions.
Step 2: Try to unlock these emotions (catharsis).
Step 3: Rationally consider the effects of these emotions (costs and benefits).
Step 4: Consciously decide to let them go.

STEP 1: IDENTIFY YOUR UNRESOLVED EMOTIONS

The counsellor helped her to explore her emotions and Carol was able to identify and acknowledge her feelings of uselessness and worthlessness, and also of humiliation, which she still felt intensely. The problem with this kind of negative emotion is that it drains your energy and it is therefore possible that you will feel you do not have the strength to face it. However, if you can gather your wits amid the storm of emotions, you may come to realise that you have no option: you simply have to face and try to resolve them, otherwise they will lead you down the road to depression.

The good news is that the counsellor helped Carol to get in touch with the same feeling of anger that she had experienced when she discovered the man's infidelity, and she prompted her to use this energy to complete her processing, to take back control of her life and to rebuild her shattered self-esteem. As a result, she felt confident enough to carry on.

STEP 2: TRY TO UNLOCK THESE EMOTIONS (CATHARSIS)

With the counsellor at her side, Carol recalled the hectic days before the break-up. She admitted that she had felt useless, worthless and humiliated by the way her ex-boyfriend had treated her. Unfortunately, these feelings had persisted even after she had ended the relationship. In reviewing the incident, her vivid memories brought back all the emotions. This caused her to start crying and the counsellor had to support and encourage her to continue. However, surprisingly, it did not take long before Carol was able to compose herself and she was ready to adopt a more rational and objective view of her situation.

STEP 3: RATIONALLY CONSIDER THE EFFECTS OF THESE EMOTIONS (COSTS AND BENEFITS)

In line with the rational approach, the counsellor urged Carol to ask herself why she was still holding on to these emotions when the incident was long past. What was the payoff or the value of doing this (if any)?

Carol recalled how her original feelings of anger had had some benefit, as when she saw him in an intimate moment with another woman. This anger had given her the strength to break free of the psychological hold he had had on her. Fuelled by the thought that he could do this to her after she had been so faithful and given up so much of herself for him, Carol had been able to take action and end the relationship.

However, by this time most of her anger had dissipated, but it had been replaced by these persistent thoughts and feelings of uselessness and worthlessness. The counsellor pointed out that there was obviously more to this issue than just the break-up, and she asked Carol about her past.

Carol explained that she had always struggled with her self-esteem, as her father had been domineering and not particularly close to her. She was an only child, and it seems that he had actually wanted a son and this caused him to largely ignore her, depriving her of his love. She recalled how she had felt this rejection as a child, which then led to feelings of self-doubt and low self-worth. So, it was quite possible that these emotions had originated in her childhood and were simply resurrected by another domineering male figure in the form of her ex-boyfriend.

The counsellor now asked her to consider the cost of hanging on to these emotions of uselessness and worthlessness. It was clear to

Carol that they were now of no benefit at all to her, just a terrible liability. The initial sympathy she had received from family and friends had quickly dried up when she became negative and withdrawn, and these feelings were certainly not helpful in her job and career.

When Carol began to weigh up the actual damage that these emotions had caused in her life, it turned out far worse than she had initially thought. They had reduced her self-esteem even further, to the point where she had lost her connection to her authentic (rational) self and had brought her to a dark place where she felt alienated from her family and friends. Even though she was free of her toxic relationship, Carol admitted that she was no longer interested in social activities and, for some unknown reason, was avoiding her old friends. Perhaps it was because they had been right all along, and she couldn't admit to it. She felt miserable most of the time and it was almost as if her whole life had turned sour. She had also become quite sickly and booked off work regularly with irritable bowel syndrome (IBS), which is a symptom of stress and anxiety.

THE TURNING POINT

However, in spite of the pain of having to relive her unhappy memories, Carol stuck to her processing and, fortunately, the counsellor was able to help her to come to a new, more insightful view and a broader perspective of her childhood as well as of the final incident (the break-up) which had brought back those self-destructive emotions (this is called 'reframing' and is discussed in more detail later).

During one moment of authentic insight – a turning point in her process – Carol realised that she had never been useless or worthless, in spite of her father's rejection and the cruel words of her ex-boyfriend. The truth was that she was intelligent, she had educated herself and had made a success of her life and career. She was certainly not the useless, worthless person that he had been telling her she was. It was now clear that her ex-boyfriend was simply the kind of narcissistic person who wanted to dominate and control others. In fact, his behaviour had been a case of gender-based violence, pure and simple.

Looking at the whole situation now with the benefit of hindsight, Carol realised that anyone with common sense could have seen that their toxic relationship would never have worked in the long run, and it was a good thing that she had been able to end it.

STEP 4: CONSCIOUSLY DECIDE TO LET THEM GO

These new insights were very important to Carol's healing. She had believed things about herself that were simply not true. Now she wanted her personal power and her authenticity back. There was simply no logical reason why she should hang on to these painful feelings. She also felt irritated by the fact that she had allowed this self-deception to take place, and this annoying thought would provide the fuel for her final step: that of consciously letting go. As in the previous case of Joan, Carol also found comfort in the fact that she was doing it for herself, not for anyone else, and for her own healing and physical health.

Carol also decided to use affirmations to assist her in her commitment to finally let go of the feelings of uselessness and worthlessness. She was also able to stand in front of her mirror at home and affirm the following:

'I was fooling myself.'
'I was never useless or worthless.'
'I now consciously let go of those feelings.'
'I claim back my personal power and authenticity.'

Over the next few weeks, Carol kept reinforcing these affirmations until they started to work at a subliminal level and she began to feel less tense, anxious and depressed. With the help of the counsellor, she also formulated and implemented a plan of action steps for her recovery. This is discussed more fully in chapter 8.

GUILT AND SELF-BLAME

Guilt is another powerful emotion that could cause anxiety and lead to depression. Let's use another case study and apply the same four-stage rational process to try to deal with these emotions.

Once again, we will use the rational tools of sticking to the truth (the facts of the incident), the power of hindsight, the process of logical reasoning (logic) and good old-fashioned common sense. If you have similar feelings, you are welcome to follow the process and apply the same skills to your own situation.

CASE STUDY

Ann was involved in an accident where she hit a pedestrian with her car and killed him. Since then, in spite of being found not guilty of culpable homicide in court, she continues to be plagued by feelings of guilt and self-blame.

Ann has had a terrible time since the accident. She had to appear in court several times, face the deceased man's family and, at the same time, deal with her own trauma from the event. This has all pushed her coping mechanisms to the limit and her emotions have taken over her life. She has withdrawn from many of her social activities and is often alone and gets caught up in her thoughts.

Her family are very concerned as she used to be a very outgoing and confident young woman and these feelings of guilt and self-blame are crippling her emotionally. The good news is that the anxiety and conflict she is experiencing means that she has not yet lost her authenticity as the situation is bothering her intensely. This is a positive sign for her healing process.

The inner conflict between Ann's conscience and her past actions has been very difficult to manage, but she knows that if she doesn't deal with it, she could spiral down into depression. She decides to use the rational (CBT) approach to healing. In this case, notice how step 3 has changed to a rational consideration of the incident itself. In any crisis situation involving strong emotions, our cognitive processes are affected and our perceptions and judgements can be biased, distorted or irrational. These errors in thinking only worsen the negative feelings.

This is also an introduction to the more advanced processes of reframing the incident and the reconstruction or reformulation of thoughts and self-talk which is applied in the second part of this chapter.

Step 1: Identify your unresolved emotions.
Step 2: Unlock these emotions (catharsis).

Step 3: Rationally consider if your guilt and self-blame are justified.

Step 4: Make a conscious decision to let them go.

STEP 1: IDENTIFY YOUR UNRESOLVED EMOTIONS

Ann is being helped by a close friend to deal with her emotions on the issue. However, in order to heal, she has to review the situation again and 'own' the feelings of guilt and self-blame.

STEP 2: TRY TO UNLOCK THESE EMOTIONS (CATHARSIS)

As before, Ann recalls the details of the incident that led to her intense response.Once again, she feels intensely guilty and is still blaming herself for his death. She releases what she can of the emotions by sobbing and expressing her regret. It is clear that she feels tremendous sorrow and sadness and she is supported by her friend. Her tears show that she is still authentic in her actions and true to her conscience and integrity.

After a while, Ann indicates that she is ready to explore her perspective regarding the incident and try to come to a better understanding and acceptance of what happened.

STEP 3: RATIONALLY CONSIDER IF YOUR GUILT AND SELF-BLAME ARE JUSTIFIED

Ann applies rational skills to achieve a more truthful view of the facts, as well as using the power of hindsight and attempting a more logical or objective, common-sense view of all the factors involved in the incident itself. (This is called 'reframing' the incident and is discussed in detail later).

WHAT IS THE TRUTH? (WHAT ARE THE UNDISPUTED FACTS?)

Ann remembers that it was dark, that she had not been drinking, that her car was roadworthy and that the victim had been intoxicated and staggering along the freeway at night. These facts had led to her being found not guilty in the court.

However, for some reason, she still lives every day with guilt and self-blame, asking herself if there was not something else that she could have done to avoid him. Or perhaps it wouldn't have happened at all if she had just taken a different route (here she is second-guessing herself).

COMMENT

The trauma of the event has skewed her perception and so she can't see that she was not to blame for what happened. It seems that the idea of killing a person, even by accident, had flooded her mind to the point where she could no longer be objective and rational about the incident. However, having kept her authenticity, she is quite willing to try the rational method of dealing with her trauma. If you are suffering from the same feelings of guilt or self-blame, try to apply her process to your own story. Let's follow Ann's thinking process as it unfolds:

> 'In hindsight, there was very little I could have done to avoid the accident.'

> 'It was night-time, and I was on the freeway travelling below the speed limit.'

'This gentleman was on the side of the road and staggered into the lane when I approached him.'

'I hit the brakes quickly and as hard as I could but I could not avoid hitting him.'

'I stopped and still tried to help him.'

'It is the thought of having killed someone that is causing me this stress and is dominating my thinking.'

In applying her mind to the facts of the matter, she now realises that nothing she did was unreasonable in view of the circumstances. She was thinking clearly and driving properly at the time. She also went as far as contacting the family and expressing her sorrow and regret. It also appears that the family do not seem to blame her. However, for months now she has been plagued by the guilt and self-blame.

Ann comes to the logical (and accurate) conclusion that it was the shock of the accident which set off the stress response and is driving these emotions. She now recognises that this is normal under the traumatic circumstances, but her guilt is not justified in view of her actions, which were reasonable under the circumstances. She has gone through the trauma of the legal processes and done what she could to resolve the matter. Thinking objectively, Ann has also come to understand that any other person would have ended up in the same situation if they had been driving the car on that road that night. She was just in the wrong place at the wrong time.

STEP 4: MAKE A CONSCIOUS DECISION TO LET THEM GO

In Ann's case there are no benefits in allowing these feelings to dominate her life. They have made her miserable and unhappy and affected the way she feels about herself and also her relationships with her family and friends. Ann understands that it is something that she regrets and will never forget, but she knows she has to learn to forgive herself so that she can get her life and happiness back. The cost of this overwhelming sense of guilt is simply something that she can't carry for the rest of her life.

Having reached a better and more positive perspective on her situation, Ann is now ready to make the conscious decision to let the feelings go as best she can. As I wrote before, when it comes to trauma it is an unfortunate fact that, although one can let go of the pain, the memories will always remain.

Ann also decides to use affirmations and stands in front of her mirror. She affirms her Authenticity and her personal regret relating to the matter, but also her commitment to letting go and to healing. She is now able to affirm the following:

> 'I have done everything I could.'
> 'I am now letting go of this guilt and self-blame.'
> 'I will no longer allow them to control me.'
> 'I am authentic and real.'
> 'I am whole again.'

COMMENT

In Ann's case her authenticity is clear: she is real and genuine in her regret and her commitment to healing. This should allow her to rebuild her self-esteem and her life again.

CHAPTER 8

A RATIONAL (CBT) APPROACH TO DEALING WITH ANXIOUS AND DEPRESSED THINKING

Before I move on to the details of the rational approach to dealing with anxious thoughts or depressed thinking, I need to show you how easy it is for errors of thinking to affect your perception of events – especially when strong emotions arise during the incident. In previous case studies, you saw how trauma, shock and strong emotions can distort a person's thinking and perspective on a situation. Unfortunately, there are quite a few other ways in which other errors can creep in too. It is these errors that we also try to deal with and correct during a rational approach to emotional healing.

The following section shows how easily different types of error can enter our thinking, especially during an unpleasant experience, and lead to or sustain negative emotions.

ERRORS IN OUR THINKING

Authenticity is linked to a clear and rational thinking mind. And, unfortunately, as human beings, we are subject to a number of possible errors in thinking. For example, our minds are typically full of biased perspectives, contradictions, inconsistencies, misperceptions, self-induced deceptions, delusions and logical errors (irrational thoughts), some of which are able to enter our minds when we are exposed to stressful situations.

Other thinking errors may simply be part and parcel of our normal thinking processes, having been formed from our past conditioning, experiences and lack of authenticity.

The assumption of the rational approach is that a correction of these errors could bring relief from unpleasant emotions and self-defeating self-talk and ultimately a return to authenticity. This, in turn, will lead to more objective and logical thinking, increased feelings of well-being, and also a new sense of meaning and purpose in life.

Let's look at a few of the common thinking errors that can prevent a return to authenticity: biased perspectives, bias, a limited perspective, preconceptions and assumptions, contradictions, inconsistencies, self-deception, misperception, errors in common sense and reasoning, and errors of logic. Each of these is described and illustrated below.

BIASED PERSPECTIVES

Everyone has their own perspective or view of the world, which can be explained as the particular way we look at and think about something. For example, we have scientists who have a purely scientific view of the world, pragmatists who are people who see things in practical terms (if it works, it is acceptable), idealists with high-minded goals who try to strive for the highest ideals, liberals who judge all actions in terms of social and human rights and religious people who view the world through the scriptures. The list goes on and on. As you can see, a person's personal perspective would be aligned with and formed by their past experiences, beliefs, level of education and value system and if they are authentic, it would reflect who they are as a person.

BIAS

Sometimes the truth or even the facts of a matter are not that obvious. Everyone views life through a personal 'lens' or perspective formed from their past experiences, beliefs, values, judgements and perceptions. And if your lens is clouded due to conditioning, attitudes or bad past experiences, your thinking could be biased and irrational at times.

The problem is that what we all see in and understand about the world when viewed through this 'lens' is naturally biased by our own perspective or point of view. In the previous sections of this book you have seen the effect of inauthenticity on one's thinking.

This natural bias in our personal perspectives means that we all have preconceived ideas about life and also conditioned responses to events, people or situations. This means that our interpretation of events or situations will be biased in some way or another.

For example, our minds can filter incoming information to the point where we see only certain aspects of an incident or situation or understand our actions only in a certain way which fits our own perspective or point of view (which is based on our past experiences, beliefs, values and even attitudes). Perspectives are not 'wrong' in the true sense of the word; they can be biased or limited, though, which can lead to errors in our thinking.

A LIMITED PERSPECTIVE

The problem is that people can have a limited perspective based on their backgrounds, circumstances or lack of knowledge and education. For example, a highly educated, wealthy, well-travelled person will have a much broader and deeper perspective on the world than a poor person living in a one-roomed shanty who is exposed only to daily suffering and misery. This is why we all end up with different so-called 'personal truths', which depend on the depth of our understanding and experience.

A limited perspective can influence a person's ability to make good decisions and can lead to consequences which only bring about further stress and anxiety. This is why it is wise always to consider all the facts, even different points of view, when making decisions. In other words, it is important for good decision-making always to engage with your rational and unbiased authentic self.

PRECONCEPTIONS AND ASSUMPTIONS

People with a limited or biased perspective will have preconceived ideas and a tendency to ignore the facts, to jump to conclusions, to make assumptions or to judge others in a stereotypical way so as to fill in the gaps in their knowledge and experience. They will see in events what they expect to see and judge things based on what they personally, with their limited experience, believe to be true.

In this world of appearances, things are not always what they seem. With social media and deep fakes, we now have more fake news and misinformation circulating out there than ever before. In other words, someone could get very upset about something which is not true at all, simply because they assume it to be true. If you combine this with the average person's limited under-standing of or perspective on the true situation in the world, people don't know what to believe anymore, and this can also lead to anxiety.

CONTRADICTIONS

Apart from the problems associated with our biased perspectives, we also have more detailed and specific problems in our thinking such as inner logical contradictions. This can be explained as believing or doing something which *clashes* directly, or indirectly by implication, with another attitude, idea or belief that we have. This points to a lack of coherent thinking, which can be a big problem when we try to make sense of a situation. For example, revisit the case study of Susan that I used previously, where she believed in a religion that was anti-abortion but her personal conviction was pro-abortion.

There can also be contradictions between what someone says and how they actually behave. And, of course, this renders their views or actions both irrational and meaningless.

CASE STUDY

Peter is a deacon in his church. He often makes the point that he believes it is important to love and accept everyone. On the surface, this appears quite wonderful and laudable. However, those who know Peter have, on occasion, also heard him make critical remarks about people of other faiths. Although he calls for universal love and tolerance, he cannot accept (or love) anyone who does not belong to his faith. This is a fundamental contradiction.

Eventually he may come to realise this or else someone else will point it out to him and he will experience the cognitive dissonance I wrote about earlier: the mental discomfort caused by the contradiction between his beliefs and his actions. At some point he will have to deal with the matter because, if it is left unresolved, it will prevent him from acting authentically in the future and it will certainly introduce doubt and uncertainty in his mind.

Contradictions are found mostly in our thinking relating to contentious matters such as morality, politics and religion, as these are complex issues with many sides, points of view and perspectives. But they can also point to a lack of authenticity, where we are not fully aware of the real implications of our thinking or actions (that is, a lack of self-awareness).

INCONSISTENCIES

Another problem in thinking is inconsistency. An inconsistency is a thought, idea or statement that simply does not 'add up' or fit into the general pattern of your thinking. In other words, what you are now thinking or saying does not make sense in the light of your actual beliefs and values.

CASE STUDY

Consider the case of Mary, who is a gentle soul who believes in the goodness of people and universal love and peace. However, Mary's life over the past week has been anything but loving and peaceful. She has been violently mugged and has had her car stolen. She is devastated, as her faith in people has been dashed. She cannot make sense of it all and this is causing a huge inner conflict between her earlier belief in people as good and the new thoughts that are going through her mind about the criminals who attacked her. This confusion will be reflected in both her anxiety and tensions and in her self-talk.

This is a perfect example of an inconsistency entering a person's thinking that could result in uncertainty, confusion and anxiety and threaten their authenticity.

SELF-DECEPTION

I pointed out previously the problem of self-deception, which can also lead to inauthenticity. For example, when talking to a person about how they are doing in their job, you may find that they tend to see themselves as more competent, experienced or qualified than they actually are in order to show off or boost their ego or false sense of self. However, anyone who knows them will say that this isn't true. They are either blind to their own limitations or deliberately trying to mislead you. As I wrote previously, this self-deception can be so strong that even if you showed them a security video of their actions, they would not admit to it or want to believe it.

Self-deception will be reflected in their thinking, self-talk and arguments, which will not fit the facts of the situation or the actual circumstances, proving that they are just fooling themselves. Unfortunately, this can lead to unnecessary emotional pain and anxiety, as they simply can't see the truth of their own situation.

MISPERCEPTIONS

Perceptions are judgements or conclusions we arrive at which have passed through the 'lens' of our minds. And, like any camara lens, the lens of our mind may well be out of focus, being based on personal factors and our biased interpretation of the facts or what we believe to be the facts or the truth of the matter.

Our perceptions can also be so badly skewed and affected by strong emotions that they are not accurate at all; in fact, they could be so out of touch with reality as to be completely wrong.

The truth of the matter is that our minds are so powerful that we can even change what we think we are seeing, hearing or reading to suit our own emotional needs, beliefs or point of view. This can easily result in a faulty perception of the important facts of an event, incident or situation and bring about a great deal of unnecessary stress and anxiety.

These misperceptions can be seen in people's thinking, self-talk and what they say, if you compare this objectively and impartially with the true facts of a particular matter.

ERRORS IN COMMON SENSE AND REASONING

It is interesting to note that judges are now basing some of their judgments on the motives or actions taken by the accused party that they consider to be irrational. This means that the person's decisions or actions do not conform to common sense, reason or logic; nor do they even indicate a proper understanding of the situation.

Such a lack of rationality can also be linked to inauthenticity. In other words, these are cases in which the false sense of self is in control and decisions are made based on self-interest without thinking about whether they are fair, reasonable or even accurate.

CASE STUDY

For instance, Clive is a senior manager who has a personal agenda, which is to further his own interests and gain a promotion. He wants to impress the directors and, against the concerns of the union, orders the workers to work double-shifts to increase production. When the workers start booking off sick, the union takes the matter to the labour court. The court supports the union and orders that Clive's decision to unilaterally impose double shifts be set aside as it is unreasonable and irrational in view of the lack of consultation and the fact that there were other ways available of increasing production.

ERRORS OF LOGIC

An error of logic is a mistake in the flow of scientific reasoning, which is the method we use to reach valid conclusions when doing research in science, psychology and other fields of study.

Logical reasoning is based on inferences: one conclusion flows directly from the previous one. However, these inferences have to be accurate and must have no 'holes' in them otherwise the outcome could be an error of logic. Consider the following example:

CASE STUDY

Trevor is travelling in a game reserve with his family and sees what he believes is elephant dung in the road and then says that this shows that an elephant has recently passed by. At first glance this seems true, as it is undeniable that an elephant produces elephant dung.

However, a logical error could still creep in. For example, Trevor may be wrong in assuming that it is elephant dung as it could be that of another large animal such as a rhinoceros, which animals are also kept in the reserve.

Let's put this into a logical form and you will the see the problem with the logic:

> Premise 1: Elephants produce elephant dung (true).
> Premise 2: There is elephant dung in the road (not necessarily true).
> Conclusion: An elephant is nearby (not necessarily true).

Trevor's conclusion is based on the assumption that it is elephant dung that he is seeing. This is not a good idea regarding the logic, as there are other possible explanations (that is, it could be the dung of a rhinoceros).

This shows how easy it is to fall into logical traps and jump to faulty conclusions if we don't have all the facts at our disposal or the full picture of a situation or an event.

This means that, when it comes to unpleasant incidents or events in our lives, especially those which produce strong emotions, it is easy to make assumptions and end up with errors of logic in our thinking. This could cause us unnecessary anxiety and distress and lead to bad decisions or wrong actions.

Learning to think logically would also be a good idea if you want to return to authenticity. In this regard, consider my other book *Critical thinking*.

CHANGE YOUR THINKING

Previously we looked at ways of reducing your anxieties and the negative feelings associated with depression to reach catharsis or a healthy release of your emotions. In this section we specifically examine how to tackle the unhelpful thinking and self-talk which underlies and sustains these emotions.

I have already shown you how easy it is for errors in our thinking to lead to unnecessary stress and anxieties in our lives due to misinterpretations, misperceptions and assumptions. If you ever wish to cope with emotional challenges and return to authenticity, you will have to learn how to deal with these errors and clear your mind to make place for authentic and rational thinking. This will help you avoid the pitfalls associated with self-destructive types of thinking and prevent you starting down the road to depression.

APPLYING THE RATIONAL APPROACH

In applying the rational approach to dealing with errors in the thinking underlying your anxiety and feelings of depression, you will have to begin by objectively examining both the truth, reason-ableness and logic of your thinking and your self-talk and actions. This was applied to a degree in the previous section on dealing with negative emotions. However, in this section we delve even deeper into the errors of thinking and also the self-talk that give rise to anxiety and feelings of depression.

The idea of the rational approach is to look more deeply and objectively at a situation after your emotions have settled down. After that can seek new insights into your actions which will support the fact that you acted quite reasonably during the incident, considering the actual circumstances. And that there may be other important factors in your favour that you overlooked or left out in your original assessment which led to a negative reaction. New insights and perspectives may help you to let go of any left-over negative feelings and allow you to accept yourself and your past actions and, ultimately, return you to authenticity.

First, as in the previous section on emotions, when evaluating your thinking and self-talk, you will be trying to get through to the actual truth of the matter. In other words, search for both indisputable facts and any deeper, hidden factors which were present, details which may have influenced why you reacted in the way you did and why you allowed the negative thoughts and self-talk to take hold in your mind in the first place. Perhaps there were elements that you didn't notice or consider when you did your immediate self-evaluation after the incident. Remember that shock and strong emotions can skew one's thinking; therefore, your original perception of the situation may have contained errors of thinking that led to your strong emotional reaction.

Secondly, once again when dealing with your perceptions, thoughts and self-talk, you will need to review the incident again. But now you should apply specific cognitive strategies to change your perspective on the incident or situation and see the new and more positive conclusions that you can come to.

Thirdly, you must look for actions which show that you acted quite rationally and reasonably in dealing with the incident and that your self-deprecation is irrational and uncalled for. An example of this would be the fact that, even under such pressure and stress, you were still able to think logically and make good conscious decisions. This will allow you to challenge and refute the negative conclusions and self-beliefs that are usually at the core of the unpleasant emotions and replace them with more self-affirming beliefs.

Finally, you apply good old-fashioned common sense to ascertain whether you are being realistic about your role in the incident and the way things turned out. As mentioned previously, the shock of a traumatic incident or accident can cause one to lose perspective and objectivity. I remember that only a few months ago I was involved in a motor-vehicle accident and received such a shock-bang to my car that for about ten minutes I did not know where I was. Fortunately, there was a lady close by who was able to help me to take down the details of the event, as I was very confused. This shows how a sudden shock to the system can cause disorientation and a misinterpretation of any event.

There are a number of steps you will need to follow if you wish to try this method:

Step 1: Identify your self-talk.
Step 2: Reformulate your thoughts about the situation.
Step 3: Empowerment: let go of any victim mentality.

STEP 1: IDENTIFY YOUR SELF-TALK

The first step is to put your anxieties, fears, worries and feelings into words and phrases. What were the first thoughts that passed through your mind during the incident? You can also do some self-introspection and identify those thoughts that persistently pre-occupy your mind even now long after the event. This would be your self-talk.

Once again, I will use case studies to show you how this is done in practice. Try to apply these techniques to your own situation.

RATIONAL (CBT) TECHNIQUES CASE #1

CASE STUDY

Wendy had a bad childhood in which she was belittled by her father for being overweight. This led to her being quite vulnerable to criticism and she now has low self-esteem.

Wendy was feeling devastated after her boyfriend broke up with her. She couldn't accept that he had left her and thought the problem was with her. This led to feelings of uselessness and worthlessness, and she was on her way to the dark pit of depression.

These emotions can be seen in her self-talk:

'I can't handle this situation. It is too much.'
'I am useless and worthless.'
'No-one will want me.'
'I may as well just die.'

With these kinds of thoughts continually filling her mind, it is no wonder that she felt anxious and depressed. She had clearly lost touch with her rational self (authenticity). As I said, it was these thoughts that were the root cause of her negative emotions and were continuing to sustain them. It was a vicious cycle which she had to stop.

Wendy read about the benefits of using a rational (CBT) approach to deal with her negative self-talk and learnt to apply her rational skills to confront these thoughts and self-talk and break the cycle before they led to full-blown depression.

Let's follow her process and see if you can copy these techniques and apply them to your own situation.

STEP 2: REFORMULATE YOUR THOUGHTS ABOUT THE SITUATION

But before we unpack Wendy's process, let's have a look at the skills she used and which you will need to learn to apply.

First, you will be trying to change your thinking away from negative ideas and self-beliefs to more positive insights and a deeper understanding of yourself as well as of the incident itself. This is not an attempt to bamboozle or fool yourself into believing and accepting new ideas that are not true, but rather an attempt to *recognise the errors in your thinking* (there will be many) that have occurred as the result of this shock reaction.

Once you recognise and acknowledge that you may have missed important details, you can use them to correct your thinking and you may find out that your role in the situation was not as bad as you originally thought.

After you correct the errors in your thinking, such as any misperceptions, assumptions or irrational self-beliefs that you originally formed in your mind, you can then let go of these misguided thoughts and your negative emotional responses to them. Doing this will set your mind at ease and put you back on the road to authenticity.

There are a number of specific cognitive skills that Wendy used and which you can also use to challenge and change any self-defeatist thinking and self-talk.

REFRAMING

Let's start with a technique called 'reframing'. Metaphorically, this would be like taking a painting out of an outdated picture frame and matching it to a much better frame that brings out the beauty and the hidden attributes of the painting. Simply put, reframing a situation means looking at it from another (hopefully more positive) point of view or perspective.

Previously, I showed you how a person's own perspective contains bias. This is why it is usually necessary to see professionals such as psychiatrists, psychologists, counsellors or life coaches when you experience emotional problems such as anxiety or depressed feelings. This is because they offer an objective view of your situation without all the filters that you have installed as a result of your background, past experiences, personal perspectives and beliefs.

When you are reframing the incident, you are aiming to reach a new understanding or a more positive interpretation of the situation without the paralysing effect of self-deprecating emotions. Hopefully some of these emotions will already have been released during the process of catharsis discussed in the previous section on dealing with emotions.

CASE STUDY

Let's return to Wendy, who, as you may remember, was dumped by her boyfriend and had strong feelings of uselessness and worth-lessness, believing that she was the problem. She had even entertained thoughts of suicide.

By now a few weeks have passed and Wendy has searched for a better understanding of her situation. She has gone through a process of catharsis, releasing some of the painful emotions, and is now trying to let go of preconceived ideas about her past relationship. She consciously reviews what she knows to be true without assuming anything. She focuses on the cold, hard facts without being pulled down by the emotions and takes a long, more objective look at the incident which led to her emotions and self-talk.

Fact number 1: Wendy accepts that she is vulnerable to low self-esteem as a result of her difficult childhood and this may have caused her to overreact to the break-up.

Fact number 2: In hindsight, she realises that the relationship hadn't been working for quite a while.

Fact number 3: Wendy also admits that she didn't set boundaries in the relationship.

Fact number 4: Her ex-boyfriend was emotionally and physically abusive towards her. This is gender-based violence and should not have been acceptable to her. It was her fear of being alone and her low self-esteem that kept her in the relationship.

Fact number 5: Drinking and drugs formed part of the problem and she admits that she was pressurised into participating.

Wendy now stands back and reframes the situation by looking at it in a logical and unbiased manner. She also considers the long-term implications for her future. She now sees that it was a doomed relationship from the outset and she was on a downward spiral towards addiction and other self-destructive behaviours.

She had effectively given up her authenticity and had created a false sense of self just to be accepted by her boyfriend and his friends; as a result, she went along with their bad habits of drinking and drugs. This had only led to further problems in the relationship.

After this period of self-examination and her re-framing the incident and her situation in this manner, Wendy's common sense tells her that the break-up was a blessing in disguise, because, by staying in this toxic relationship, she was heading for even more serious problems. She also understood that it was better that the breakup occurred in the early stages of their relationship, because, if they had been married and had possibly had children, the situation would have been far more complicated and painful.

RESTRUCTURING YOUR THOUGHTS AND SELF-TALK

In psychology this technique is normally called 'cognitive restructuring'. This is yet another skill or approach in which you tackle and dismantle each line of negative thought and self-talk and rebuild your line of thinking with more positive self-affirming insights.

LET'S APPLY THIS APPROACH TO WENDY'S CASE, SPECIFICALLY HER LINES OF SELF-TALK

'I can't handle this situation. It is too much.'
'I am useless and worthless.'
'No-one will want me.'
'I may as well just die.'

During her rational approach to healing, Wendy also re-examined each line of her negative self-talk. And after her emotions had settled, she could see that these beliefs were simply not true – or at the very least irrational nonsense.

For instance, the first truth was that she had actually been coping with her home and work situation after the break-up. She found her own flat and was still working normally. In other words, the first line in her self-talk suggesting that she couldn't handle the situation was actually not true at all. It was her emotional upset that was the problem.

The second truth she came to accept was that she was in a senior position at work, doing very well financially and a great asset to her company. The self-statement that she was useless and worthless was therefore a total misperception. It was the shock of the break-up, combined with her vulnerability to low self-esteem, that had led to her self-talk of being useless and worthless.

The third untruth she believed was that no-one would want her. Looking logically at her situation (and with hindsight), she realised that she had been very popular with her friends and family before her relationship with this ex-boyfriend and that she had enjoyed her life. It was clear that it was he who was making her feel inse-cure. In other words, this idea of her being unpopular and that no-one would want her is totally irrational in view of the facts relating to her previous social life.

Finally, Wendy logically reviewed the fourth line of negative self-talk: her believing that she just wanted to die. The process suddenly became a bit scarier. This line suggested that she had labelled herself as a *victim with no power* to change her situation. This is a dangerous state of mind, as was seen in the section on victim mentality. Although, as before, the shock of the break-up had created this line of self-talk as a reaction to her pain, this was something that she still needed to deal with.

STEP 3: EMPOWERMENT: LET GO OF VICTIM MENTALITY

Having an authentic self means that, at your centre, you are an empowered person with choices and not a victim of your past circumstances. You have to internalise this truth, because, unfortunately, if you have a bad experience or a series of them and are not careful with your thinking, you may begin to see yourself as a 'victim' and this can lead to deeper emotional issues. This is what had happened to Wendy.

LET'S NOW APPLY THIS TO WENDY'S CASE

With her emotions having settled down and after a more common-sense look at her situation, Wendy quickly realised how absurd this thinking was. It was absurd in view of the fact that this was only a single incident in her life, something which happens to everybody. And it was certainly not severe enough for her to label herself a victim or to consider suicide.

As a result of her rational processing, Wendy was able to deconstruct all the lines of her negative self-talk and was able to reconstruct and reformulate her thinking and self-talk into more positive and self-affirming beliefs about herself. Doing so enabled her to rebuild her self-esteem and return to authenticity, as seen in her new affirmations.

She had also taken back her personal power and now felt sufficiently empowered to consciously let go of the idea of being a victim. As a final gesture, Wendy stood in front of her mirror and affirmed her new sense of self:

'I am now letting go of these untrue and irrational
thoughts about myself.'
'I will no longer allow them to control me.'
'I am not a victim but a winner.'
'I am authentic and real.'
'I am whole again.'

RATIONAL (CBT) TECHNIQUES CASE #2

Now let us consider a second, more detailed case study which will give you greater insight into the details and power of the rational approach.

CASE #2

Here we have the case study of Ralph, who was hijacked at an intersection by a man with a gun and simply handed over the keys to his car. This type of situation, in which someone faces the possibility of death, is actually *trauma* and a worse-case scenario, but Ralph's case provides us with a good example of how to do cognitive restructuring to set the matter straight. This is the kind of process you will have to follow.

The background to the case is that, after the incident, Ralph was on the road to depression due to lingering feelings of guilt, worthlessness and uselessness. He believed that he should have fought back and not passively handed over the keys. This resulting in his believing himself to be a coward and useless as a man. Fortunately, after a few weeks, he recovered sufficiently to challenge his initial thinking and was able to stop himself from going into depression.

Let's now note the rational steps that Ralph followed to get back his self-esteem and personal power and help himself to get back on the road to authenticity.

In this case we again have to assume that Ralph has already had a period of adjustment in which he acknowledged his feelings, was able to explore and express them, and reach some degree of catharsis. This is necessary to enable his thinking to be more rational.

Again, here are the three steps to take when dealing with errors in your thinking and self-talk:

Step 1: Identify your self-talk.
Step 2: Reformulate your thoughts about the situation.
Step 3: Empowerment: Let go of any victim mentality.

STEP 1: IDENTIFY YOUR SELF-TALK

Let's follow Ralph's train of thought and self-talk and see how he managed to reformulate his thinking using a rational approach and to get back on the road to healing.

Ralph was able to identify and record his self-talk as follows:

'I should have done something other than just handing over the keys.'

'I did nothing. I was a helpless victim.'

'I am useless and worthless.'

STEP 2: REFORMULATE YOUR THOUGHTS ABOUT THE SITUATION

As can be seen, Ralph's traumatic experience affected him profoundly and resulted in a train of self-talk that became progressively worse. This is typical of a descent into depression. Your self-talk gets worse until you believe that you have nothing left to live for.

REFRAMING

Ralph began by using the technique of reframing to get a new, broader perspective on the incident and to look for reasons why he behaved in the way he did. Follow the steps he took and see if you can apply them to your own situation.

Ralph began by examining the unbiased truth of the incident without the burden of the powerful emotions, which had settled down to some extent after a few weeks. The first question he asked was this: What were the facts that influenced my actions?

Fact number 1: He was alone in a vehicle on a deserted road.

Fact number 2: He was faced with a determined hijacker armed with a gun who knew what he was doing and possibly would have had no hesitation in killing him.

Fact number 3: There was no other help available and no way of getting help if he had been wounded.

He summed up his real-life situation as follows:

'I was alone in the car and under threat of death from a lethal weapon.'

His perspective on the situation is quite accurate, as the truth of the matter was that there was not much that he could have done when faced with such a dangerous situation.

In hindsight, Ralph admits that he knew the danger he was in and that this influenced the actions he took. It was a case of his survival instincts kicking in. Even after reviewing the incident objectively, he could not see any other option open to him.

What was important was the fact that he had actually been thinking and considering his options during the incident. In the few moments that were available to him, he had considered climbing out of the car and fighting with the hijacker. However, he came to the conclusion that if he had not been able to over-power him, he would be shot and there would have been no going back.

After thinking logically about the incident, he asked himself this question: Would any reasonable man have taken that chance?

In fact, he recalled that there had been a lot of support for his actions. After the incident when he had discussed the matter with the police, they had told him that compliance is the best course of action during a hijacking if the perpetrator has a firearm, and also to get away from the car as soon as possible to avoid being taken as a hostage. In Ralph's case, he had taken both these steps: he had given up the keys and moved away from the vehicle.

After this rational review, Ralph has a new perspective on the situation. He now realises that he actually did very well. He did not panic or do anything stupid. He was thinking rationally in spite of the highly tense situation. His feelings and negative self-talk are merely the result of the shock and trauma of the event.

RESTRUCTURING YOUR THOUGHTS

To conclude his rational re-evaluation of the event, Ralph puts his new insights into action and tackles his self-defeating self-talk head on using cognitive restructuring.

Follow the process and see if you can apply these steps to your own situation:

'I should have done something other than just handing
over the keys.'
'I did nothing.' 'I was a helpless victim.'
'I am useless and worthless.'

In taking line one of his self-talk, Ralph concluded that his rational review had shown him that there was not much he could have done other than simply handing over the keys. So he realised that his original line of thinking was irrational in view of the actual danger and circumstances of the event.

When it comes to line two of this self-talk, he now realises that, in fact, he did do something and was not helpless. He remembers that he was thinking rationally at the time, even though it was a tense situation, and had realised that if he handed over the keys and moved away from the car, he would prevent a possibly worse outcome. For example, he knew that the hijacker could have taken him as a hostage and driven him around the whole night, emptying his bank accounts, and that his chances of surviving after that would have been nil. Line two of his self-talk is then totally false, too.

The same applies to line three, the belief that he was useless and worthless. The measure of control that he had over the situation refutes this. This line is false in view of the fact that his actions indicated rational thinking and a plan to rid himself of the hijacker as quickly as possible in a safe manner.

As a result, he is able to change his perception of the past situation. He now believes that when he thinks logically about the dangerous situation he was in, he did the best that he could under those circumstances.

As a result of this new, more reasonable, realistic and positive view of the past incident Ralph is able to understand that his negative self-talk was simply triggered by his powerful emotions. As a result, he is now able to move on to the final stage of letting go and reconstructing his thinking and self-talk relating to the incident altogether.

STEP 3: EMPOWERMENT: LET GO OF ANY VICTIM MENTALITY

From his self-talk, we can see that Ralph originally saw himself as a helpless victim. However, after careful and in-depth rational consideration, he could now see that this was never the case.

The fact that he had made a conscious decision to get out of the situation – which was to get rid of the hijacker as soon as possible by getting out of the car, handing over the keys and then moving away – indicated that he wasn't as helpless as he had initially thought. He had a simple plan to get out of the situation, although, at the time, it felt as if he did very little to help himself.

However, this was caused by a twisted misperception of his true actions due to the effects of the trauma.

Ralph now feels that he can now let go of this negative self-talk relating to this incident.

He now stands in front of the mirror and makes new commitments:

> 'I make a conscious decision to let go of my negative self-talk.'
> 'I am not a victim but a survivor.'
> 'I am authentic and real.'
> 'I am whole again.'

In being able to reconstruct, reformulate and change his thinking and self-talk to more positive and self-affirming beliefs and ideas, this allows Ralph to accept himself and his actions, rebuild his self-esteem and, finally, return to authenticity.

CHAPTER 9
A PLAN TO HELP WITH ANXIETY AND DEPRESSION

A cognitive-behavioral (CBT) approach to healing demands a plan in which you have to be prepared to make changes to your lifestyle, your day-to-day activities, your attitudes and your patterns of thinking in order to return to authenticity. Remember that much of your stress is due to inner conflict and strong repressed emotions such as anger, guilt and feelings of despair, and that, by taking steps to resolve them, you can ease your anxiety.

A well-defined plan will also deal with those issues, thoughts and self-talk that are sustaining your feelings of depression. So, in the case of both anxiety and depression, a plan of simple action steps is necessary.

Having a plan will also give you the direction and confidence to move forward and take more responsibility for your life. Taking personal responsibility for your actions is also a sign of being authentic. If you apply your plan, you will be able to think more rationally, independently and clearly, be more in touch with yourself and accept that you have matters to deal with. It is this rationality and clarity, and the confidence that you are back on the road to recovery, that will help you to continue with your plan.

A good counsellor will not impose a plan on you but should allow you to put together your own plan for change based on your personal situation according to what is possible for you. For instance, not everyone has the finances or the opportunity to make major changes to their lifestyle, so in your case a series of steps which fit your own circumstances, goals, needs, possibilities, strengths and weaknesses is fine, as long as you are moving forward and are prepared to implement them.

In the following section I have given you a few ideas as a guide, but it is up to you to decide on what you can manage on your path back to authenticity.

THE THREE PHASES OF THE PLAN

Phase 1: Lifestyle changes
Phase 2: Your day-to-day activities
Phase 3: Changes to your attitude to life

PHASE 1: LIFESTYLE CHANGES

SIMPLIFY YOUR LIFE

To return to authenticity, you need to get back in touch with yourself. *Create the time and space* for balance in your life by simplifying your lifestyle, cutting down on distractions and simply spending more quality time with yourself and your family. You can't expect to become more authentic and reduce your level of anxiety if your life is filled with the constant pressure of demanding work or, alternatively, it comprises a mad rush to parties, going out pleasure-seeking and living excessively.

It makes sense that you will experience stress and anxiety if you follow a lifestyle that does not suit your personality and vulnerabilities. Start by remaining true to your needs as a 'real' person and not pursuing some grandiose idea of being in the glamour of celebrity culture.

SPEND TIME IN NATURE

Go away regularly at weekends and spend time with your family, especially in outdoor settings. Quality time spent in natural surroundings can reduce anxiety: the fresh air and the greenery have a soothing effect on the mind. Spend more time doing nature rambles, walking along the beach or even hiking in the mountains. The exercise will also serve to keep you healthy and take your mind off your concerns. This will work well for both anxiety and depression.

LOOK TO YOUR EATING HABITS

A good diet can help to combat both anxiety and depression. For example, complex carbohydrates work to maintain a balanced blood sugar level, and this can keep you calmer. Drink plenty of water and avoid alcohol and caffeine (which is a stimulant).

Avoid processed foods and eat more natural foodstuffs such as whole grains, fruits and vegetables. There are many new fads out there such as intermittent fasting. The problem is that this practice causes your blood sugar to drop, and low blood sugar could worsen your anxiety.

REDUCE UNNECESSARY DEMANDS ON YOUR TIME AND PROTECT YOUR PERSONAL SPACE

Protect your private time and personal space. Don't make unnecessary commitments. Focus your attention on those activities which you are drawn to, especially those that bring you joy and satisfaction.

If you feel uncomfortable and stressed when you are invited to be on school boards or the committees of clubs or the boards of non-governmental institutions, accept that this is not who you are and refuse the invitations. It may be only my own experience, but I have found these boards and committees to be dominated by forceful personalities who can be a source of interpersonal irritation for you. You don't need that in your life.

Speaking of interpersonal conflicts, try not to be pulled into other people's arguments, emotional dramas or matters which don't really concern you. Just withdraw discreetly. You are not being difficult, just authentic about not wishing to become involved.

People who feel depressed will naturally avoid social interaction as a coping mechanism. Hopefully, your mood will improve with time and you will feel strong enough to interact at least a little again.

KNOW AND AVOID YOUR TRIGGERS

Both anxiety and the emotions associated with depression could have triggers. By now you should know those situations and issues that stress you the most. Try to avoid them as much as possible.

- For instance, driving at night is stressful for me due to my night-blindness, and this means that my wife drives me around after dark.
- If you feel insecure in certain areas of your city, avoid them.
- If you find yourself in a toxic work environment, try to arrange to work more from home (online or hybrid work).

CASE STUDY

Susan took early retirement due to a toxic work environment. After a few months at home her anxiety subsided and she was coping quite well. Then Susan was offered a part-time job, but her new boss insisted that she come into the office every day. After doing this a few times, she began to feel uncomfortable and stressed again and realised that this was not what she wanted. She had no hesitation in giving up the part-time work as it was simply not worth the stress of travelling in busy traffic early each morning and working under the direction of a demanding boss again. Her new, more authentic approach to life helped her to realise that her mental health was worth more to her than the extra income.

WATCH OUT FOR THE SMALLER TRIGGERS TOO

This sounds trivial, but images of violence, whether on the news or in television programmes, can play on your mind and cause you unnecessary anxiety. For this reason, stay away from ultra-violent films on television and on the big screen.

If the news upsets you, reduce your viewing time. Rather look for more light-hearted entertainment. This applies especially to persons who feel depressed. This is not a case of burying your head in the sand. Realising that you are in a vulnerable space and don't need that kind of negativity in your life is actually being authentic.

BE MORE PRAGMATIC IN YOUR APPROACH TO WORK

Let go of perfectionism because it can place great demands on a person and will definitely lead to anxiety if there is a sudden over-load or things don't go as planned. A reasonable and mindful person will adjust their expectations of themselves to fit their work circumstances. A constant overload could also push you to the point of *burnout*, and you may eventually go into a form of depression as a result.

CASE STUDY

James is a supervisor at an engineering firm and he has always been a perfectionist. He takes his work very seriously, is very dedicated and always tries to help everyone to get the job done. He never says no, even if he is expected to do extra work.

Unfortunately, over the past few months, his workload has increased dramatically, and he finds that he is running around like a headless chicken trying to keep up with the demands. This is stressing him to the point where it is affecting his ability to think clearly and also influencing his emotions adversely. It has got so bad that during a rush of work he has panic attacks in which he stutters and acts like a bumbling idiot.

What his fellow workers don't realise is that his state of mind is actually due to his level of commitment and his efforts to get everything done perfectly, even if things go wrong or sudden and unreasonable demands are placed on him.

Eventually his boss sends him to a psychologist, who listens carefully to his story and comes to the conclusion that James is a perfectionist who tries to get all the work out even under almost impossible conditions.

James learns a valuable lesson from the psychologist, one which helps him to cope and function better: 'to do the best you can within the prevailing conditions.' In other words, he still does his best, but if the conditions suddenly change and there is an overload, he is satisfied that he has done his best even if everything is not completed in the time frame given.

So the message from James's case study is a simple one: simply do the best you can under the prevailing conditions and leave it at that. If your boss is unreasonable, just tell them you are doing your best. Getting chewed on is less of a problem than ending up in an institution with an anxiety disorder or depression.

LEARN TO SAY NO!

When it comes to your work, bosses will often flog a willing horse and you could end up carrying too much of a load while others sit around doing nothing. In other words, you will have to learn to speak up and say 'No!' if you feel you are close to your stress limit. Be authentic and accept that you have a problem with stress and anxiety. Just refuse and say 'Sorry, I can't do that at the moment as I am already running with a full load'.

You may find that little 'cheats' can also help to reduce your work-load and also your tension level. For instance, find out what you can do to delegate some of your workload to others and find ways of doing things that help you to cope better, such as working from home some days.

CONSIDER A CAREER CHANGE

It sounds drastic, but one day you may have to make a decision that determines whether you will literally live or die. The worst-case scenario is that you may have to change career paths to find one that is more suitable, as a stressful and toxic work environment is one of the main causes of anxiety and depression. Trust me on this: I have been there!

CASE STUDY

Casey was in a high-powered human resources position. He had been promoted to deputy director and was appointed to the position of chief negotiator with four worker unions. The company was experiencing many labour problems and this kept him very busy, with the result that he could not give attention to most of his other tasks.

Although he had a great position, the demands were excessive and he was no longer enjoying life at all.

Casey began to experience anxiety and had a number of health issues, especially problems with his stomach. This eventually led to his undergoing corrective surgery.

Later, when it came to promotion, Casey was overlooked and replaced in his position, which caused him even greater anxiety — this time about his future. By now his work situation had become even more toxic and eventually he took the decision to leave the company and take early retirement.

Since then, Casey has recovered and he has taken on a completely different path, doing some part-time work, mostly online. His anxiety is now manageable and he once again enjoys life. He now realises that leaving the toxic work environment actually saved him, as he was heading for a major physical and emotional break-down. In other words, authenticity may come at a cost, yet it typically leads to a richer, more complete life.

FOCUS ON MORE RELAXATION

MUSIC

Music has been shown to affect a person's mood. I would recommend that you listen to relaxing music when you feel a bit anxious and stressed. Alternatively, uplifting and inspiring music could also help you when you experience feelings of depression.

BREATHING EXERCISES

There is a technique called diaphragmatic breathing that involves consciously taking slow, deep breaths with your belly rather than your chest to reduce anxiety. This is necessary because people who are anxious often hyperventilate, taking rapid shallow breaths which can lead to an increased heart rate (causing more anxiety) or light-headedness.

SPORTS AND HOBBIES

Your plan could include new hobbies or sports such as golf or fishing, where you have the time to spend outdoors in nature, which will have a positive effect on your feelings of well-being. I have found fishing to be very relaxing and it will certainly take your mind off your concerns for a while. This relaxing type of activity also helps for depression.

Hobbies are also a great distraction that help to take the focus off your daily worries. Painting, drawing and writing (eg short stories, poems or a memoir) can give you an additional sense of satisfaction, which will also help to improve your mood and help with depression, as such creative activities give you meaning and purpose.

If you are young and fit enough, even more rigorous sports such as gym, running or walking would be beneficial to countering both anxiety and depression, because the activity releases tensions and generates those feel-good hormones too. Sporting activities can also be quite sociable, which can lead to your making new friends, which can also help to distract you from your concerns and at the same time give you a degree of fulfilment, especially when you begin to observe an improvement in your performance. Once again, witnessing such positive changes can help to resolve depressed emotions by giving you a new sense of purpose.

SLEEP

Also make sure that you get plenty of sleep. Being sleep deprived will render you even more irritable and anxious. Depressed people do tend to sleep a lot, though, so, in this case, try to work out some suitable programme that enable you to rest, but not all the time. You need to get out of the house at least once a day for a walk or a drive to the shops, otherwise you could start feeling worse as a result of sitting at home the whole time.

PERSONAL GROWTH COURSES

For those of you with the time and finances, I would recommend that you enrol for a structured personal growth course. If you look online, you will find many such courses being offered. I would suggest in-person group courses, as you will receive the face-to-face support you need from others who are also wanting to learn how to deal with life's challenges. This step will work well for both anxiety and depression.

LIFE COACHING

If your anxiety is not yet a major problem or you don't want medication or to see a doctor, psychologist or psychiatrist, consider engaging the services of a life coach. Life coaches can help you to clarify your goals, identify the problems you are experiencing in your life (such as anxiety), and then help you to come up with strategies to deal with the issues causing your anxiety.

Life coaches can also advise you on how to make the most of your strengths and coping mechanisms and give you the support you need to progress on your upward curve of personal development. It has become an increasingly popular way of getting support for day-to-day stressful living.

Life coaching may also help you to deal with your feelings of depression, although in the case of clinical depression it should be combined with a supervised programme of medication.

SUPPORT GROUPS

If your anxiety has reached a level where you need more support, consider an anxiety support group. This step will also apply in the case of depression.

A support group is a group of persons who share a common past experience which has affected all of them in a negative way and they come together for the purpose of sharing their stories and supporting one another.

Usually, some have metaphorically already passed through the 'dark valley' and they are willing to pass on their accumulated wisdom and coping skills to others in the group who are still struggling to come to terms with their negative thoughts and emotions.

Examples of support groups are groups for people with HIV/Aids, single parents, victims of gender-based violence, rape victims and alcoholics – and, of course, anxiety and depression groups. Such groups provide a 'safe space' for members to unburden their feelings and thoughts by sharing their experiences and getting the support of a counsellor and other members of the group.

Use your online resources and search for an anxiety support group in your area. In this country you can contact The South African Depression and Anxiety Group (SADAG) at https://www.sadag.org/. I am sure there are similar groups in your country too.

PHASE 2: YOUR DAY-TO-DAY ACTIVITIES

The question here is what you can do daily in a practical way to improve your authenticity and reduce your anxiety when having to deal with everyday life challenges. These steps can be applied whether you experience anxiety or feelings of depression because they bring back structure and control into your life and daily activities.

In these cases you need to make a commitment to follow these steps and stick to them, pretty much like new year's resolutions.

TAKE MORE RESPONSIBILITY FOR YOUR LIFE

Begin to take more personal responsibility for your actions. Simply admit to yourself that you made a mistake and work towards correcting it. Remember John's case study and the problem of self-deception or fooling yourself. This is related to a reluctance to take responsibility and points to immaturity and also a lack of authenticity.

Look more carefully at your role in challenging situations and make a conscious effort to stop blaming others for your problems, anxieties or lack of advancement. Accept that your emotional vulnerability and your own actions may have played a part in the situation you find yourself in. An authentic person will admit when they are wrong and learn from the lesson.

BRING YOUR BEHAVIOUR BACK INTO LINE WITH YOUR TRUE FEELING AND VALUES

Begin to act in ways which match your true feelings, values and needs and let go of criticism or the fear of rejection by others. Begin to recultivate those activities that are indicative of authentic living – such as genuineness, letting go of masks and airs, being totally honest, having a non-critical, non-judgemental approach to people, returning to your core values and cultivating a genuine concern for others.

'I was raised to treat the janitor with the same respect as the CEO.'

TOM HARDY

LET GO OF MASKS AND AIRS

By now you should've seen how wearing masks to impress or deceive others leads to a lack of authenticity. Although, in the short term, you may gain acceptance, respect or prestige from pretence, lies and deception, in the long term it erodes your personality, isolates you from yourself and leads to anxiety, as you know that you may be exposed at any time.

BE HONEST

Be honest with yourself and others from the beginning. Let go of your illusions and self-deception and strive for the clear conscience that goes with being transparent in your dealings with people. People like and respect others whom they experience as honest, sincere and genuine.

FOCUS ON YOUR RELATIONSHIPS

Commit to being open and honest in your relationships too. Also try to be less judgemental and more unconditionally accepting of others. Each person has their own past history and set of problems and they all deserve our patience and support. Often, we do not know what they are dealing with at home.

Robin Williams is quoted as saying, 'Everyone you meet is fighting a battle you know nothing about. Be kind. Always.'

Don't be afraid to show your vulnerability, compassion and concern. Just make sure that they are genuine feelings, not just a show. Try to build true empathy by volunteering to help others whenever possible.

Second, authenticity means that you are not biased towards any religion, creed or culture, and this means being fair and treating all persons equally.

LET GO OF TOXIC EMOTIONS

I mentioned that some of your anxiety may be due to leftover emotions such as anger, bitterness and resentment due to what happened to you in the distant past. This is understandable, and no one here is judging you because of it. However, for the sake of authenticity, you have to continue with the battle until those emotions have been resolved.

Using a rational approach to healing means that you have tried to come to terms with your situation using a process of reasoning and a number of rational skills. However, I won't repeat all these steps as you were shown how to do this in the previous chapters. One of your action steps could involve continuing with the self-help techniques until you can safely let go of these toxic feelings.

PHASE 3: CHANGES TO YOUR ATTITUDE TO LIFE

A simple change in your attitude could give you back your meaning in life and help you on the road back to recovery and, ultimately, your authenticity. Changing your attitude means re-evaluating your beliefs and reframing your perspective on the incident and on life in general; it can also entail seeing if there are any factors previously hidden from your view which could make things clearer for you. Let's reconsider some of these areas.

REVISIT YOUR PHILOSOPHY OF LIFE

In a previous section I showed you how important meaning and purpose are for someone who is losing hope and can't see the way forward when faced with depression. A good action step for helping with both anxiety and depression is to re-evaluate your view of life and look for the positive in what you have. An optimistic feeling of gratitude is a powerful counter to negative emotions.

Have a look at this case study, which shows both the pain and the growth of someone who has reevaluated their life and come to more positive conclusions simply by changing their perspective and philosophy of life.

CASE STUDY

This is the case study of Jamie, whose severe bout of depression made him slow down, pause and reconsider his life and discover what was really important to him. This is what Jamie had to say:

'During this dark period in my life, even my values, religious beliefs and spirituality came into question. My beliefs had been the foundation of my sense of meaning, security, self-acceptance and identity, and when they were uprooted by such a traumatic experience, for a while I become lost, alienated, fearful and angry at everyone, including life itself. In fact, I began to question and re-evaluate my own sense of self.

'However, during this time of deep self-questioning, I came to understand a number of profound personal truths and gained new insights into my life and purpose.

'With my old beliefs and preconceptions of the world being shattered, I was left empty. This opened me up to a new, broader understanding of life. For example, it was important for me to discover that even this sense of loneliness and abandonment had a purpose, as it brought with it the time and space for reflection on my deepest doubts and fears. I also realised that the pain of this experience had been an opportunity to empty myself of my ego and to come to know my authentic self or spiritual centre.'

COMMENT

By accepting what had happened to him and starting over again, Jamie found a new path, one which was less focused on the attractions and distractions of the world and more on service to the community. He joined a non-governmental organisation and began his work of helping those in need. During this time of service Jamie regained his authenticity and found peace, fulfilment and a deeper understanding of what his true purpose in life is: to use his skills and time to help others and to become what he was capable of becoming. The process of self-actualisation often takes place in service to others.

LOOK FOR NEW PERSPECTIVES ON YOUR PAST

Try to look at your past situation from different points of view. A new perspective may be just what you need to help you put those unpleasant experiences behind you. For example, look at the following case study.

CASE STUDY

Jill was overlooked for promotion and the position was given to a more junior member of the staff. This upset Jill very much and she became angry and bitter, believing that she was a victim and the company was working against her. However, at the same time, the company's approach changed and Jill soon realised that this promotion would have put her in the position of implementing policies which would have compromised her ethics and values, and which would have gone against her conscience.

In hindsight, she is now grateful that she did not get the promotion as she, at least, has retained her integrity and authenticity and realises that this is more important than her advancement in the company.

A CHANGE IN PERSPECTIVE?

Perhaps there was a good reason for that unfortunate event in your own life, or perhaps it could even have been an opportunity to grow?

- If you are a spiritual or religious person, could this have been a lesson in humility?

- Even if you are not spiritual, could this have been a lesson in the need to focus on the right priorities in your life? (depression empties the ego)
- Didn't you need to slow down a little? Perhaps you were overly driven and it could have ended badly. It may be that you needed time for rest and self-introspection.

CONSIDER A NEW METAPHOR? TRY VIEWING LIFE AS A CLASSROOM

Has your metaphor for life changed at all? Was this not a wake-up call or a lesson to be learnt? Sometimes we miss seeing the value in the new insights we have gained. Perhaps, as part of your plan for recovery you could change your view of life to one of its being a place of learning, a classroom, in which the setbacks become lessons that you have to learn. Life is full of challenges and tests which we all have to complete, but that's how we grow.

LOOK FOR A LARGER PURPOSE IN YOUR LIFE

I think we are often so blinded by our own needs and ambitions that we fail to realise that the world does not revolve around us as individuals. Once we willingly empty ourselves, or are forced to do so while experiencing depression, we open ourselves to new insights and levels of understanding.

There are many great teachers out there who have themselves had the most horrendous experiences and yet they turned their lives around to teach and help others in the same situation. You have been put here on Earth for a reason. Nature doesn't act without a purpose. Everyone has a role to fulfil. Perhaps you just haven't discovered yours as yet.

Possibly this experience you went through was preparing you for something bigger, some important work you still have to do. If I can give you a tip based on my own experience, this work does not involve your gaining anything except a sense of fulfilment by reaching out and helping other people.

FINALLY, CONSIDER THE FOLLOWING

We are here for each other. We are all part of one humanity in which the person with one eye will help others who are blind. In this case, I have found that becoming involved in charity work and giving back to the community is a useful way of learning to be humbler, more empathetic and more generous. There are always those who are worse off than us and would welcome a helping hand. Doing this will take the focus off yourself and allow you to change your attitude to one of positivity and gratitude for your own life.

CONCLUSION
BUILDING RESILIENCE

It sounds a bit strange that you may come out of a bout of anxiety or depression stronger and more resilient than before, but it is possible. A broken state of mind is like a broken bone which, when it heals, can be stronger than before. This is so because you've had to develop new coping skills and build resilience in order to manage your condition.

Conditions such as anxiety and depression can be opportunities for self-examination, self-reflection and gaining new insights. Perhaps you were pushing yourself too hard, driven by ambition or a striving for success. A bout of depression will put the brakes on anyone chasing after money, fame or performance, because it brings you down to earth with a bang!

Taking time off and being at home gives you the opportunity to gather your resources and to rest, and this can be positive if you use the time wisely to discover who you are.

Depression means that you have reached the end of your rope. Somewhere along the line you have taken on too much or over-extended yourself. Sometimes you simply need time to rest and gather your thoughts and also to make new and better life choices.

Unfortunately, if you don't consciously deal with the matter, you could lose yourself in the experience and your state of mind may spiral down into full-blown clinical depression. In this case, the chemical changes in your brain can be long-lasting and you might find it difficult to recover. However, let's look on the bright side and trust that there will be light at the end of this dark tunnel.

If you're able to use the information and skills I have showed you in this book, hopefully you should be able to return to authenticity and have a better understanding of your true abilities, coping skills and purpose in this life.

Over time, if you adopt a more philosophical and meaningful approach to life, you will be empowered to let go of life's daily little irritations and regain the drive to be perfect in everything you do. Authentic thinking should also make you more resilient to any future challenges.

I hope that this guidebook on dealing with the effects of anxiety and depression has been of some use to you. It was compiled and has been passed on to you with genuine love and concern. Remember that you are a child of the Universe and that there is a plan for your life.

Let me conclude with the following quotation which I think sums it all up perfectly:

'Someday, everything will make perfect sense, So, for now, laugh at the confusion, smile through the tears, be strong and keep reminding yourself that everything happens for a reason.'

JOHN MAYER (AUTHOR AND MUSICIAN)

I wish you all the best in your great work. I hope this book has been of benefit to you.

For more interesting articles, please visit my website www.discoveringyourself.co.za

Dr Jimmy Henderson

SOURCES

BOOKS

Barlow, D.H. & Durand, V.M. (2002). *Abnormal psychology: An integrated approach.* (3rd ed.). Belmont: Wadsworth/Thompson Learning.

ONLINE SOURCES

https://www.helpguide.org/mental-health/treatment/therapy-for-anxiety-disorders

https://www.clinicalpsychologisthd.co.za/true-self-and-fals/

https://www.verywellmind.com/live-with-authenticity-7483232

https://www.psychologytoday.com/za/basics/authenticity

https://www.merriam-webster.com/dictionary/authentic#:~:text=1,own%20personality%2C%20spirit%2C%20or%20character

https://www.google.com/search?q=rational+approach+in+psychology

https://www.medicalnewstoday.com/articles/326738

https://positivepsychology.com/authentic-living/

https://dictionary.cambridge.org/dictionary/english/congruence

https://www.apa.org/topics/anxiety

https://www.healthline.com/health/alienation

https://greatergood.berkeley.edu/article/item/seven_ways_to_find_your_purpose_in_life

https://ptspsychology.com/wp-content/uploads/2021/08/Why-Being-Authentic-Matters_SSalicru.pdf

https://www.psychologytoday.com/za/blog/more-feeling/202101/anxiety-authenticity-and-the-art-not-being-poser

https://www.merriam-webster.com/dictionary/self-deception

https://www.shortform.com/blog/inauthentic-behavior/

https://www.bustle.com/p/15-little-signs-you-arent-being-fully-authentic-every-day-73784

https://lup.lub.lu.se/luur/download?func=downloadFile&recordOId=8968604&fileOId=8968605

https://www.stanfordchildrens.org/en/topic/default%3Fid%3Danatomy-of-the-skin-85-P01336?undefined

SOURCES

http://klinicka.nakladaslap.com/public/pdf/2017-2.pdf

https://www.researchgate.net/publication/333136493_Authenticity_and_Its_Adaptive_and_Maladaptive_Relations

https://www.tutor2u.net/psychology/topics/congruence

https://www.frontiersin.org/journals/public-health/articles/10.3389/fpubh.2022.986531/full

https://www.hopkinsmedicine.org/health/treatment-tests-and-therapies/how-to-help-someone-with-anxiety

https://www.medicalnewstoday.com/articles/existential-anxiety#:~:text=Existential

https://www.mentalhealth.org.uk/our-work/public-engagement/mental-health-awareness-week/anxiety-report/what-causes-anxiety

https://www.mind.org.uk/information-support/types-of-mental-health-problems/stress/causes-of-stress/

https://championhealth.co.uk/insights/anxiety-statistics/

https://theconversation.com/depression-anxiety-and-childhood-trauma-south-african-study-explores-links-prevalence-and-whos-most-at-risk-196058#:~:text=To%20estimate%20probable%20anxiety%2C%20we,African%20respondents%20had%20probable%20anxiety.

https://www.sjp.co.uk/media-centre/latest-news/feeling-the-strain-increasing-financial-stress-takes-its-toll-on-mental-and-physical-health-of#:~:text=Ongoing%20financial%20strain%20is%20taking,James's%20Place%20(SJP).

https://psychopathyis.org/what-causes-psychopathy/

https://www.saferspaces.org.za/understand/entry/gender-based-violence-in-south-africa

https://www.verywellmind.com/anxiety-and-self-esteem-1393168

https://www.healthline.com/nutrition/12-benefits-of-meditation

https://www.webmd.com/diabetes/low-blood-sugar-anxiety-link

https://www.sadag.org

https://www.sadag.org/index.php?option=com_content&view=article&id=1836&Itemid=167

https://www.uofmhealth.org/conditions-treatments/digestive-and-liver-health/diaphragmatic-breathing-gi-patients

https://medlineplus.gov/ency/imagepages/19529.htm#

https://www.youtube.com/watch?v=cXy6VE6PoGQ

https://web.cortland.edu/andersmd/rogers/self.html

https://depthcounseling.org/blog/winnicott-true-false-self

https://www.verywellmind.com/live-with-authenticity-7483232

https://www.google.com/search?q=existential+anxiety+meaning

SOURCES

https://www.mind.org.uk/information-support/types-of-mental-health-problems/anxiety-and-panic-attacks/symptoms/ (2023)

https://www.linkedin.com/pulse/power-authenticity-how-embracing-who-we-can-promote-cara-mcnulty-dpa/

https://www.psychologytoday.com/za/basics/self-talk

https://mg.co.za/news/2023-10-18-broke-and-stressed-south-africans-spiral-into-debt-trap/

https://www.saferspaces.org.za/uploads/files/Integrated_SCP_Strategy_0.pdf

https://www.google.com/search?q=anxiety+statistics+in+south+africa&

https://theconversation.com/depression-anxiety-and-childhood-trauma-south-african-study-explores-links-prevalence-and-whos-most-at-risk-196058#:

https://www.google.com/search?q=anxiety+and+health&

https://www.mayoclinic.org/diseases-conditions/high-blood-pressure/symptoms-causes/syc-20373410

https://www.mayoclinic.org/diseases-conditions/generalized-anxiety-disorder/symptoms-causes/syc-20360803

https://www.statssa.gov.za/publications/P0211/Media%20release%20QLFS%20Q2%202024.pdf

https://my.clevelandclinic.org/health/diseases/9536-anxiety-disorders

https://hcpc.uth.edu/pages/wimi/anx.htm#:~:text

https://www.verywellmind.com/what-is-a-life-coach-4129726

https://www.health.harvard.edu/blog/nutritional-strategies-to-ease-anxiety-201604139441

https://www.google.com/search?q=how+to+cope+with+anxiety&rlz=1C1MSIM_enZA912ZA912&oq=how+to+cope+with+anxiety&

https://www.sciencedirect.com/science/article/abs/pii/S0092656621000416#:~:text=with%20ultimate%20meaning.-,Abstract,in%20multiple%20aspects%20of%20meaning.

https://psychcentral.com/lib/stop-irrational-thoughts

https://web.facebook.com/permalink.php/?story_fbid=431687156575775&id=100092034833689&_rdc=1&_rdr#

https://depthcounseling.org/blog/winnicott-true-false-self

https://www.britannica.com/science/self-actualization

https://www.mayoclinic.org/diseases-conditions/depression/symptoms-causes/syc-20356007

https://www.jax.org/news-and-insights/jax-blog/2015/december/happy-or-sad-the-chemistry-behind-depression#:

https://www.sciencedirect.com/topics/psychology/emotional-contagion#:

SOURCES

https://www.lesswrong.com/posts/sWGQDdoWwyE7qhRif/the-competence-myth

https://www.psychologytoday.com/intl/blog/the-age-of-overindulgence/202308/developmental-affirmations-that-may-change-your-life

https://www.nimh.nih.gov/health/topics/depression

https://www.verywellmind.com/what-is-a-victim-mentality-5120615

https://my.clevelandclinic.org/health/treatments/25067-exposure-therapy

https://www.collinsdictionary.com/dictionary/english/persecution-complex

https://www.verywellmind.com/what-is-catharsis-2794968

ABOUT THE AUTHOR

Dr Jimmy Henderson has a PhD in Psychology from the University of South Africa and a certificate in trauma counselling. He is a chartered people-practitioner who specialises in Learning and Development (CHRP 5049).

Dr Henderson has done volunteer counselling and training for 40 years, four of which entailed offering trauma counselling to staff of a well-known South African banking group.

He espouses a person-centred approach to life, his focus is on personal empowerment (helping people to help themselves) and he is the published author of a number of self-help books. In his books he uses analogies and both hypothetical and real-life case studies together with psychological research to explain difficult concepts in a simple and understandable way. This adds to the uniqueness of his books.

He is very focused on the notion of being fully authentic and believes that a loss of authenticity lies at the heart of many personal problems and, in some cases, can even contribute to conditions such as anxiety and depression. He uses these as focus areas for this book.

His life experience, when viewed in the light of his intensive studies and counselling work, gives him a very broad base of practical knowledge which should be useful to those seeking a better understanding of how to regain their authenticity, rebuild their self-esteem and give new meaning and purpose to their lives.

This guide could also be useful for counsellors, life coaches, caregivers and support organisations who work with those suffering from anxiety or depressed feelings.

TESTIMONIAL

'He shares from the heart and his approach is put across very clearly; it is very understandable.'

PILIANA

ALSO BY THE AUTHOR

Let me also invite you to have a look at my other books and e-books, which are on Amazon and on other sales platforms.

IN SEARCH OF THE ORACLE

This book contains a story about a student's passage up a mountain to search for a master or guru but is actually a metaphor for the inner journey each of us must take to discover our higher selves. It is full of imagery and symbolism and contains deep messages obtained from the master when he is consulted by a number of students and questioned about life and death, purpose, reality and God. It also describes a meditation technique used to gather the knowledge from the guru or higher self.

LIVING ON THE EDGE OF DARKNESS

This book provides insight into the mind of someone who has suffered from depression and relays a subject matter that is topical in a society where many people lose their way, suffering similarly from depression and need guidance. It provides guidelines for coping, but also highlights the journey of self-discovery of the author, in which he wrestled with many questions such as 'Who am I really?'; 'What is actually going on in the world?'; 'What is real? and 'What is the true meaning of suffering, life and death?'

UNDERSTANDING METAPHYSICS: HOW PSYCHOLOGY CAN EXPLAIN METAPHYSICAL EXPERIENCES

Book 1 in the series 'Explaining Metaphysics'

Dr Henderson takes a pioneering step forward as he puts into scientific and psychological concepts the ideas and experiences linked to metaphysical processes. By sharing his personal experiences as well as those of other practitioners, he aims to give you a refreshingly direct answer as to how it all works. The knowledge is written and presented in a manner aimed at deliberately challenging your present thinking and helping you to grow.

In this book he explores a number of crucial questions:

1. What is metaphysics?
2. How is metaphysics useful for everyday thinking?
3. How to reprogramme your mind
4. A new view of the mind and the idea of one universal consciousness
5. The development of new and powerful mental skills
6. Unlocking the power of your subconscious mind

JOURNEY TO THE SOUL

Book 2 in the series on 'Explaining Metaphysics'

This book uses a framework of metaphysics to explain the existence of a soul and the authentic self. The processes described then take you on an inner journey to break free of the limits of everyday thinking and discover the depths and possibilities of your own mind. The aim of the book is to provide you with the tools to first reconnect with your authentic self and then with your essence or innermost being, your soul itself.

UNDERSTANDING REALITY: TAKING A NEW LOOK AT WHAT IS TRULY REAL

Book 3 in the series on 'Explaining Metaphysics'

Cognitive scientist Dr Jimmy Henderson combines up-to-date scientific research with psychology, sociology and even symbolism, semantics and metaphysics to explain the latest ideas about what reality is and how it was created. The characteristics of energy form the underlying foundation of the book and he uses the systems approach in psychology as a framework to show how these energies can directly and indirectly affect us at all levels and even provide answers to the meaning and purpose of life.

The human element is also dealt with by showing the important role of our minds in forming our sense of reality.

This is a book for the serious thinker, but it is written in a very easy-going and simple style, with plenty of metaphors and analogies to help the reader understand some quite difficult new ideas on reality and even alternative realities. It will give you plenty of food for thought to enable you to formulate your own opinions.

TRAUMA COUNSELLING: AN INTRODUCTORY GUIDE TO SHARPEN YOUR PRACTICAL COUNSELLING SKILLS

This book is a good introduction for trauma counsellors, clearly describing the stages of trauma and providing a detailed view of a simple five-stage outcomes-based trauma counselling process. It also contains many practical tips and case studies to provide greater insight into the processes.

A COMPREHENSIVE GUIDE TO CRISIS COUNSELLING (2nd EDITION)

This is a full-length book based on the guide with the structured seven-stage, outcomes-based counselling process, but it contains much more background information plus training in specific areas of counselling, such as telephone, online and on-site counselling. It also contains additional sections on couples counselling, family counselling, large group counselling, suicide threats and how to run a support group.

CRITICAL THINKING: A NECESSARY SUPERPOWER IN TODAY'S WORLD

This book shows the importance of critical thinking for all areas of your life and teaches you the following skills:

- It will help you to become authentic again by cultivating mindfulness, the ability to reason effectively, to think clearly and to apply common sense and logical thought.
- You will learn how to identify and challenge false and misleading information.
- You will be empowered to see through deception, scams, dodgy business deals or dubious persons with hidden agendas.
- You will learn how to overcome your doubts and fears by building your confidence.
- Finally, critical thinking is a tool to help you to become aware of your own selective perception, prejudice and bias and to reach a fully authentic version of yourself.

SHORT GUIDES (E-BOOKS)

EFFECTIVE LISTENING SKILLS FOR COUNSELLORS AND CARE-GIVERS

This guide discusses the processes involved in active listening and will be a great asset to those involved in the caring professions.

HOW TO INTERPRET YOUR DREAMS

This guide explains the nature and reason for dreams and also shows the reader how to interpret their own dreams.

IMPROVING YOUR RELATIONSHIPS

This guide shows the reasons for the breakdown of relationships and gives guidance on how to repair broken relationships.

A GUIDE TO EFFECTIVE PARENTING

Based on current research, this book provides guidelines to both prospective and existing parents on how to raise children effectively.

A COMPREHENSIVE GUIDE TO CRISIS COUNSELLING

This short e-book guide outlines a structured seven-stage outcomes-based counselling process that is a great training manual for lay counsellors and caregivers. It was a best seller when first published and has received great reviews.